CINDY

PRAYER
90 DAYS WITH GOD

by
Bearpaw

"WHATEVER you do, do it All for the glory of God."   1 COR 10:31

Luke 10:27

xulon PRESS

Please do not be offended because of my writing style. I have chosen to write this book in the second person, using "you" instead of "me", "we", or "us". My purpose of this book is to help you, fully knowing and understanding that we all need help. In this case, "It IS all about **you**!"

www.xulonpress.com

Dedicated to the honor and glory of God;
Father, Son, and Holy Spirit.

Be faithful in prayer.
Romans 12.12

Table of Contents

Introduction xi
Day 1: Day Won! 14
Day 2: Just the Facts 16
Day 3: The Heart of the Matter 18
Day 4: Why Pray? 20
Day 5: RESOURCES – The Bible 22
Day 6: Where to Start 24
Day 7: Habits of Prayer 26
Day 8: Discipline 28
Day 9: Love 30
Day 10: The Tortoise & The Hare 32
Day 11: Statistcs 34
Day 12: The Praying Man 36
Day 13: The Praying Woman 38
Day 14: I'm Only a Kid 40
Day 15: Bearpaw Samples: Beginning Prayers 42
Day 16: When to Pray 44
Day 17: Where to Pray 46
Day 18: Humility 48
Day 19: How to Pray 50
Day 20: Talk to Me, Johnny 52
Day 21: Who Am I? 54
Day 22: What to Pray For 56
Day 23: God's Will 58
Day 24: What Is God's Will? 60
Day 25: Pray for Who? 62
Day 26: Bearpaw Samples: Prayer Lists 64
Day 27: So Many to Pray For! 66

Day 28: Supplications 68
Day 29: Petitions 70
Day 30: One Month! 72
Day 31: Intercessions 74
Day 32: I'll Be Praying for You 76
Day 33: Healing 80
Day 34: Hindrances 82
Day 35: Styles - Types - Components 84
Day 36: A.C.T.S. 86
Day 37: Confession 88
Day 38: Confession 2 (faults) 90
Day 39: Forgiveness 92
Day 40: Body Positions 94
Day 41: Create Your Own Style 96
Day 42: You're Not Alone 98
Day 43: Pharisee? 100
Day 44: Scripture 102
Day 45: Excuse Me! 104
Day 46: Popcorn Prayers 106
Day 47: 5 108
Day 48: Be Quiet! 110
Day 49: Lectio Divina 112
Day 50: Prayer Beads 116
Day 51: Psalms 118
Day 52: The Lord's Prayer 120
Day 53: Adoration 122
Day 54: The Prayer of Jabez 124
Day 55: Prayer of St. Francis 126
Day 56: Praise/Thanksgiving 128
Day 57: Sing Praises! 130
Day 58: Sing Praise! 2 132
Day 59: Book of Common Prayer 134
Day 60: Day 60 136
Day 61: The Jesus Prayer 138
Day 62: The Bearpaw Prayer 140
Day 63: Let's Eat 142
Day 64: How Long to Pray 144
Day 65: Trust Me 146
Day 66: God Is With You 148
Day 67: Fasting 152
Day 68: Did You Hear That? 154

Day 69: Recalculating.. 158
Day 70: Unanswered Prayer? 160
Day 71: Praying Out Loud 162
Day 72: Technical Support...................................... 164
Day 73: Journaling... 166
Day 74: A Note to God.. 168
Day 75: Devotionals 170
Day 76: Worship.. 174
Day 77: Father's Love Letter.................................. 176
Day 78: Scripted Prayers.. 178
Day 79: Instant Prayers/Substitution Prayers......... 180
Day 80: God or Jesus?.. 182
Day 81: The Holy Spirit... 184
Day 82: Prayer vs. Satan.. 186
Day 83: Come, Follow Me! 188
Day 84: Walk to Emmaus 190
Day 85: Ever Thought About. . . .? 192
Day 86: Sin ☹.. 194
Day 87: Don't Be a Quitter...................................... 196
Day 88: Reflection 198
Day 89: Bearpaw Samples: Closing Prayers........... 200
Day 90: The End... 202

Introduction

First and foremost, thank you for your interest in developing or improving your relationship with God through active, regular prayer. It is my hope that the following 90 day short course in prayer leads you closer to our loving God and creates a daily habit of communicating with Him.

Please understand that I am an ordinary person, like most of you, who feels there is more to worship and a relationship than merely attending church every week, or occasionally. I am not ordained, or a pastor; I am just ordinary me. So, the next 90 days may include ideas or suggestions that do not meet your "style". I get it – and I understand my style might not fit your needs. But I hope there will be enough alternatives offered to do one thing, to bring you closer to Christ!

My real name and identity is not of importance. Therefore you will see the "name" Bearpaw used throughout this book. That is my nickname, what my friends have called me since 1978. I am not seeking fame by producing this book. My personal intent is to come closer to my Lord and God and at the same time offer opportunities for others to do the same.

I encourage you to underline or highlight things that seem important to you and/or write notes as reminders of significance to you. Do your best to incorporate these ideas into your daily prayer. If after a while, you feel they do not meet your needs or you have new priorities, scrap them or modify them to your satisfaction. Eventually, you and God will come up with a plan that fits you both.

The concept for this book is that each day you read the assigned devotional; meditate, pray, and consider trying the idea. Each day will offer more and new ideas for your consideration.

By the end of 90 days, you should have a good plan for your future prayer life. Remember, no plan is perfect and no plan is permanent. At the end of 90 days or even yearly, go through the book again; this time underlining or highlighting in a different color. This is your book, a work book if you will, so use it to help you.

This book is written in the belief that God is in fact the Holy Trinity; that God sent His Son Jesus from heaven to earth as a human; and that Jesus died and was raised from the dead by God for the forgiveness of our sins. So, as I speak of God, I am also speaking of Jesus and the Holy Spirit. . . God, three in one.

This book is not designed for you to "find" God, although it is certainly possible for some to find answers about Christ they have been searching for. The true intent of this book is to offer ideas, tips, and suggestions to create or improve your worship and relationship with God through prayer.

Because there are so many facets and components of prayer, it will take 90 days to develop a full understanding of the proposed prayer concept. Each day of this journey will add to the last, and thus will take time to consider the many elements to be presented. Don't rush through the book. Take time each day to reflect on the suggestion for the day. Think about how you can most effectively apply it to your life. Meditate on the icons (pictures) scattered throughout the book; they may help you focus on the prayer aspect of the day.

For those who have been occasionally praying or even praying regularly, it is my hope that you too will find ideas in this book that will enhance your prayer life. Anyone who prays certainly realizes that prayer continually changes with experience, confidence, maturity, and time.

Research says most repetitive tasks take 21 consecutive days of activity before it becomes routine. This of course varies with the individual and the complexity of the task. Developing a "habit" of prayer is not complex, but does require discipline and commitment. It should take you 90 days to complete the book. In doing so, you will have completed 90 consecutive days of prayer and will be well on your way to establishing a routine of prayer.

Nothing in this book is exhaustive. The contents are really relatively basic in knowledge and skills. I do not have all the answers to every question you may have. I do, however, hope I have included enough information in this book to help you get started in a life of prayer or to motivate you to dig deeper for a closer life with Christ our Lord. If an idea or suggestion leaves you in question, I urge you to research the thought deeper to meet your personal needs.

So mentally prepare yourself to give time each of the next 90 days to God. Make a true commitment to give prayer a fighting chance. I can assure you that there will be obstacles presented to you along the way, that's just how Satan works. Fight back; be strong. . . just do it!

Day __1__

Day Won!

M ost of us still live with only the slightest understanding of the most ancient, dynamic source of power there is – the power that comes from prayer.[1]

This will be a slow, steady process in developing your life of prayer. The first few days are informative, slowly building into more and more prayer time and various considerations for your prayers. Be patient, it takes time to lay a good foundation. Let's get started.

Each day:

1. Go to a private place where you will not be disturbed or interrupted.
2. Plan on being alone with God for 5-10 minutes. It does not matter if your "actual" time is more, or even less. . . just plan on time with God.
3. Welcome God as He joins you.
4. Tell God whatever is on your mind – no rules, no format, just talk.
5. When you are finished, YOU WIN! Tell God "thanks" for being with you and make plans to meet again tomorrow.
6. Follow this format for the next few days, keep it simple.

The following song is my recommendation for you to listen to as you read the following covenant. Personally, I created an iTunes account and have a library of music on my computer and iPod. However, you can listen to the music in any format you choose. Throughout the book you will see the music/cross icon as a reminder to consider the suggested song as you pray.

Draw Me Close To You by Kathy Troccoli

A covenant - I promise:

My loving God, I want so much to come closer to You. Today I promise to give the next 90 days to You in prayer. In these days I ask You to open my heart to allow Your inspiration of communication to dwell within me. During this time together make me ever aware of Your presence with me. In anticipation and joy of our time together. Amen.

Note to self

_____
_____
_____
_____
_____
_____
_____
_____
_____
_____

Day _2_

Just the Facts

G od is no doubt eager and pleased to hear your prayer requests. But be assured, He does not need your requests to be informed of your needs. He knows all (this is the definition of "omniscient"). Prayer is for you! Prayer is your expression of love, trust, and faith – and is offered to strengthen the relationship between you and God. Your prayers will NOT change God, but just may change you!

You will never have pure enough motives, or be good enough, or know enough in order to pray rightly. You simply must set all these things aside and begin praying.[2]

The goal of your spiritual growth is to become more like Jesus; and Jesus spent a lot of time in prayer. Based on Scripture, one can deduce Christ prayed for approximately four to five hours every morning or at other times.[3] The man who does not pray cannot possibly be called a Christian.[4] Prayer is your declaration of dependence upon God.[5] Sadly, prayer for many is little more than sitting in a pew for an hour or so on Sunday morning - possibly saying a prayer or two. For most, the thought of prayer never enters your mind until you are faced with a critical situation or need of some sort. Equally as sad are those that recite in some mechanical form prayers learned by rote during their childhood days. Their performance of said "prayers" is most often just a case of memorization without thought or meditation on the words being said. The prayers of these people, and unfortunately they include far too many who call themselves Christians, are for the most part superficial with very little investment in creating a relationship with God.

Prayer is not something you have to do, it is something you get to do. It is not getting what you want, but rather getting what God wants for you. It is the greatest privilege of your life, part of an obedient lifestyle. Prayer is not to make your life easier, nor to gain magical powers, but to know God better.

Finally, do not compare your prayer life with that of someone else. You are unique to God and He has a unique plan just for you. He wants to take you just as you are and help you discover your own rhythm of prayer and develop a style of prayer that maximizes your relationship with Him. God desires your prayer life to be natural and enjoyable. He wants your prayer to be honest and heartfelt, and He wants your communication with Him unencumbered by rules, regulations, and obligations.

> O Lord, I ask, even in my lack of prayer power, to be made more like You. Teach me Your ways of prayer.

Know This:

You can be as close to God as you want to be; it all depends on the time you are willing to invest in the relationship.[6]

Note to self

_____

_____

_____

_____

_____

_____

_____

_____

_____

_____

_____

MIRACLES
HAPPEN
WHEN
WE PRAY

Day 3

The Heart of the Matter

J oyce Meyer says the greatest mystery of prayer is that it joins the hearts of people on earth with the heart of God in heaven.[7] The heart of prayer is prayer from the heart.[8]

Your prayer should not be looked upon as an obligation, for truly it is a privilege to talk with the Creator of the universe. Prayer is communion with God from your heart and mind.[9] These words tell us very clearly that true prayer comes from the heart, not merely words we utter to fill time and space. Prayer which is found in the tongue only will not please God; it must be found in the heart – the heart must be lifted up and poured out before God.[10]

So, the first step in approaching God in this holy activity is getting **your** heart "in shape". You must get your heart and mind ready to go to the holiest of places – God's heart. As you begin your prayer time, take a moment to think about the miracle you are about to encounter. . . you are about to talk to God, the creator of EVERYTHING (the creator of all things is defined as "omnificent")! And know this, He will be next to you and He will hear every word and thought you utter. Are you ready for that?

Do you only seek God's help when times get rough? You're probably not alone. Too many of us rely on our own skills to manage our problems. So, when you can't come up with a solution, you ask God for help. And He will help! However, God may not give you a quick fix. Instead, He may begin with your heart. Instead of merely putting a patch on your problem, He may go much deeper and examine your heart and motives

18

"The Lord does not look at the things man looks at. Man looks at the outward appearance, but the Lord looks at the heart" (1 Samuel 16.7). The Bible makes many references about God looking at man's heart. In the Bible the heart signifies the spiritual core and foundation of a person, it does not mean the physical heart. The Sovereign Lord told Ezekiel, "I will remove from them their heart of stone" (Ezekiel 11.19). Of course, God was not implying He would actually remove the hearts of those from Israel. Instead He was talking about a "heart transplant". He would remove the hardness of their hearts and fill them with repentance, compassion, loving, and forgiving hearts.

Remember this. . . .

As you grow in your friendship with God, never forget that your relationship is based on who He is and not on what He can do for you. Keep seeking His presence, not His presents; keep seeking His face, and not His hand.[11]

Ask yourself:

Is my heart in shape?
Do you need a heart transplant?
Then pray. . . .
"Search me, O God, and know my heart" (Psalm 139.23)

Note to self

_____

_____

_____

_____

_____

Day _4_

Why Pray?

You are reading this book, so there is an internal "reason" for why you are desiring to pray. Good for you! Most will agree that prayer is a key part of living in expectation of entering the kingdom of heaven.[12] The very fact that you are praying is an acknowledgement that God exists and that you need Him."[13] Indeed, if you want to pray, you are already praying.[14]

Jesus said, "When you pray. . ." (Matthew 6.6); this passage implies that personal prayer is to be the duty and practice for all believers in Christ – that prayer is not an option. God aches over our distance and pre-occupations. He mourns that we do not draw near to Him. He grieves that we have forgotten Him. He weeps over our obsession with muchness and manyness. He longs for our presence.[15]

If God knows everything about me (omniscient), why do I need to pray to have my needs met? God encourages us to pray in order to build an intimate relationship between Him and you. He is interested in much more than merely meeting your needs; He also wants to become your source of strength in every trial. Directing your prayers towards God and trusting that they will be answered according to His will and timing strengthens our awareness that without Him, we can achieve nothing. God can certainly meet your needs without a single word from you, but then you would never know the wonder of asking and receiving in love![16]

Prayer is entering into relationship with God so we can determine His will for us.[17] Your goal should be to come closer to Christ by having an honest conversation with Him every day. There is nothing, absolutely nothing, sweeter than knowing you have touched the hem of His garment in prayer[18] (see Luke 8.42-48). To seek His face and become more like Jesus is your ultimate goal. Truly, the main purpose of prayer is not to make life easier, nor to gain magical powers, but to know God.[19] With this in mind, remember that authentic prayer is not formed out of the attitude that "I should pray today," but rather from the frame of mind that "I want to be with God and I need His help."[20]

"Devote yourself to prayer" (Colossians 4.2). This passage and Ephesians 6.18-20 are the two fullest descriptions Paul gives of an all-around prayer life that is disciplined to count effectively."[21] But. . . if you are praying because Jesus expects you to, or out of guilt, or in hopes of gaining favor or special treatment – well, you are missing the point. I hope and Jesus hopes you are praying to God out of love, respect, and adoration – not because you have to (or are you a Pharisee. . . just following the law)?

Prayer within your church is also critical. The ministry of prayer is the most important of all the ministries in the church. Prayer creates the atmosphere and binds the powers of darkness so the gospel of Jesus can go forward.[22] But as valuable as that may be, it is no substitute for knowing Him, communicating with Him, and developing a personal relationship with Him.[23]

"A call to prayer is far more than a polite and consoling gesture. The greatest gift we have to offer one another is indeed our collective prayer – not merely kind wishes, not simply good intentions, but deep prayer – the ability to hold, tangibly and intentionally, others in that abundant love that flows freely and gracefully within us and among us. This has substance. This has weight and heft. This, and this alone, is the source of deep healing, lasting transformation, and enduring peace. This is our inheritance and our gift – living water for ourselves and for a world that thirsts for life."[24]

The Right Reverend Robert O'Neill,
Bishop of the Episcopal Diocese of Colorado

Day 5

RESOURCES
– The Bible

There are hundreds of Books about prayer available for you to read. All would be good to read. However, there is one Book that prepares the heart for true and honest prayer more than the others, and that Book is the Holy Bible. Know this—the greatest Book on prayer is the Bible.[25] A tremendous blessing awaits you every day in the Word of God! When you read the Bible with a sincere desire to hear God and to take His truth to heart by faith, you will receive favor from Him.[26]

So, as you can see, prayer also requires time of study – especially in the Bible. Your prayer time may be a "set time in the morning" and your time of study may be "in the evening" – or perhaps they will be done concurrently. It matters not how you choose to do them, but it is important that you do both. You will not know your Father or His ways intimately unless you are a diligent student of His Word.[27] The more time you spend reading the Bible, the more your personal life is transformed. Your focus on life and your response to daily activities will be different. You will act differently, and you will pray differently. Your power in prayer is the Word of God.[28]

The study of the Word and prayer go together.[29] The Word of God is the basis, the inspiration, and the heart of prayer.[30] Your goal should not be set by the opinions of people, not by what they say, but by what the Scriptures say.[31]

"Blessed is the one who reads the words of this prophecy, and blessed are those who hear it and take to heart what is written in it" (Revelation 1.3). It is a privilege not only to read the Scriptures ourselves, but to hear them read by others who are qualified to give us the sense of what they read and to lead us into an understanding of them.[32] Let Scripture saturate your mind and heart.[33] "Apply your heart to what I teach" (Proverbs 22.17).

There are a number of Bible translations available, choose the one you feel most comfortable with.

NASB New American Standard Bible (1971; update 1995)
AMP Amplified Bible (1965)
ESV English Standard Version (2001)
RSV Revised Standard Version (1952)
KJV King James Version (1611; significantly revised 1769)
NKJV New King James Version (1982)
HCSB Holman Christian Standard Version (2004)
NRSV New Revised Standard Version (1989)
NAB New American Bible (Catholic, 1970, 1986 (NT), 1991 (Psalms)
NJB New Jerusalem Bible (Catholic, 1986; revision of 1966 Jerusalem Bible)

NIV New International Version (1984)
TNIV Today's New International Version (NT 2001, OT 2005)
NCV New Century Version
NLT[1] New Living Translation (1st ed. 1996; 2nd ed. 2004)
NIrV New International Reader's Version
GNT Good News Translation (also Good News Bible)
CEV Contemporary English Version
Living Living Bible (1950). Paraphrase by Ken Taylor. Liberal treatment of 'blood.'
Message The Message by Eugene Peterson (1991-2000s)

BIBLE

Basic **I**nstruction **B**efore **L**eaving **E**arth

Day 6

Where to Start

Effective prayer requires focus, attention, and dedication. It becomes easier with daily offering, but initially there are a lot of decisions to be made. Do not worry about having "every detail" in place today. During this 90 day journey we will address your questions and hopefully establish a routine of daily prayer that works for you. We are all different individuals made by God. He knows the prayer plan that is best for you. Ask Him to lead you there.

There are no shortcuts. This book will offer opinions, Scripture, tools, models, ideas, suggestions. . . but you need to spend time with God. Together the two of you will develop a style of communication that best fits you. Do not compare yourself with others. People pray in different ways. Everyone has their own style. I certainly do not do everything in this book and would not expect you to do so either. Explore different ways of praying until you find the one that fits you.

The length of time required to form a habit depends on the person and the desired habit. Some say it takes 21-28 consecutive days, others say it takes up to an average of 66 days. Suffice it to say, the 90 day commitment you are making is a good start to what I hope is a life-long passion.

Andrew Murray said, "Prayer is so simple that even the feeblest child can pray, yet it is at the same time the highest and holiest work to which man can rise. It is a fellowship with the Unseen and the Most Holy One!"[34]

Prayer is the greatest privilege of your life. It is not something you have to do; it is something you get to do.[35] Make this investment a priority to establish and expand your relationship with God. Go to your place of prayer and get to know Him better.

Just Do It!

Get alone with the Father and know He is waiting and eager to have time alone with you! Remember that your relationship with Him is saturated in love. Therefore, nothing that you do or don't do can separate you from God's presence (paraphrase: Romans 8.38-39).

Note to self

_____
_____
_____
_____
_____
_____
_____
_____
_____
_____
_____
_____
_____
_____

Day __7__

Habits of Prayer

So many aspects are involved in serious, meaningful prayer. Following are some of the habits you should consider.

Discipline
Obedience
Focus
Sincerity
Honesty
Trust
Reverence
Humility
Forgiveness
Perseverance
Faith
Patience

Many of these habits will be addressed throughout this book. Some, however, will not, so I encourage you to grow through your own study of prayer as well.

Praying is far more than simply bending the knee and saying a few random words. Praying is divine.[36]

Be willing to change or modify your prayer habits occasionally. Otherwise, it may become boring. Keep it fresh and exciting.

The entire person must pray; the whole person—life, heart, temper, mind—is in it. All vain, evil, and frivolous thoughts are eliminated, and the mind is given over entirely to God; thinking of Him, of what is needed, and what has been received in the past.[37]

He who would pray, must obey. He who would get anything out of his prayers, must be in perfect harmony with God.[38] Put simply, disobedience of God is sin, and sin is not acceptable to God.

Honesty in your prayers is vital. The One who created the universe and made you knows your past, present, and future. The very attempt to hide something from God is folly.[39]

Father God, I ask so many things in prayer, but if it is not Your will or Your time, I trust You to do what is best. Through this 90 day study, I ask that You develop within me the habits of honest and effective prayer that You desire.

 In His Time by Diane Ball
Ecclesiastes 3.1

Note to self

_____
_____
_____
_____
_____
_____
_____
_____
_____
_____
_____
_____
_____
_____
_____
_____
_____

Day 8

Discipline

Good for you! You have been praying now for a week. Although there are many questions yet to be answered, one thing you have discovered is that a dedicated prayer life requires discipline. No one said it would be easy, but a close relationship with our God is worth the sacrifice.

My friend Randy has the best analogy for the progression of becoming a prayer warrior I have heard. He says, "When you first start praying your efforts are very <u>mechanical</u>, almost awkward. The days go by as you put your skills into <u>practice</u> and slowly you begin to develop a <u>routine</u>. This routine turns into a <u>habit</u> and eventually into a <u>desire</u>. As you fine tune your skills and your relationship with God becomes intimate, you realize your prayer time has become a <u>passion</u>, something you cannot live without."[40]

Being disciplined about your prayer time requires you to make some important decisions and commitments. The first, and possibly most important, is to acknowledge that you need to come closer to Christ. That is possible only by developing and strengthening your relationship with Him. To foster your relationship, you need and must spend time in prayer. Taking time out of your daily life is not easy. You are probably finding all kinds of excuses to skip your prayer time. We'll talk about this in a few weeks. In the meantime, stay focused and vigilant.

The next phase of discipline comes in developing a daily routine of reading from your Bible.

Consider spending a few more minutes each day in prayer to God. Praying for what is on your mind is always good, but now add a few specific topics. The topics of interest to most people are family and jobs. These prayers could include healing, general health, safety, patience, guidance, and of course your prayers for them to be drawn closer to Christ. Speak freely, openly, and honestly to God.

For the next week or so, pray in this fashion:

1. Go to your uninterrupted place of prayer.
2. Spend a minute or more in silence.
3. Acknowledge God's presence with you.
4. Pray for whatever is on your heart.
5. Pray for your family and friends.
6. Thank God for listening to you.

Loving God,

Be patient with me as I seek to be more like You. My attempts of conversation with You may seem awkward and uneasy, but I know You understand my intent and You know my desires without my even asking. Give me courage to continue this journey with You. Give me strength to conquer Satan and his attempts to interrupt this relationship. I love You and I thank You for Your presence with me always.

Note to self

_____
_____
_____
_____
_____
_____
_____
_____
_____
_____
_____
_____

Day 9

Love

Your discipline of prayer is a habit that God anticipates and eagerly awaits each day. But your prayers will not influence His love for you, regardless of how fervent they are, how long they are, or how much you sacrifice to give time for Him. There is nothing you can do to make God love you more. His love for you is eternal. He loved you before you were born, He loves you every minute of every day, and He will love you throughout eternity!

"Neither death nor life, neither angels nor demons, neither the present nor the future, nor any powers, neither height nor depth, nor anything else in all creation, will be able to separate us from the love of God that is in Christ Jesus our Lord" (Romans 8.38-39).

So, remember this when things do not work out as you planned, and you wonder if God loves you. . . or, He doesn't give you what you asked for and you think He might be withholding His affection. . . God loves you infinitely, and thus forgives you completely and saves you thoroughly. He is an extreme God of extreme love.[41] In God's eyes, you are worth the best that heaven could offer – the gift of His precious Son.[42] "For God so loved the world that he gave his one and only Son, that whoever believes in him shall not perish but have eternal life" (John 3.16); now that is extreme love!

Although you cannot really grasp how much God loves you, I think you get the idea that His love is far more than you or I could ever imagine. His love is so overwhelming that you will not comprehend it until the day you meet Him in heaven. But just how much do **you** love God? There are a number of things you are commanded to do in the Bible, and all of them are important. However, one commandment stands greater than any of the others. My personal signature passage of Scripture says, "Love the Lord your God with all your heart and with all your soul and with all your strength and with all your mind, and, love your neighbor as yourself" (Luke 10.27). "All the Law and the Prophets hang on these two commandments" (Matthew 22.40). Did you get that? **LOVE** of God and our neighbor sums up the 613 laws of the Old Testament. OKAY, I can hear you saying right now, "I love God!" But stop and think about it – no, really, THINK about it. . . how much do you love God?

You can't earn your way into heaven or purchase God's love with your deeds. Therefore, approach Him in your prayer life for what it is. . .an authentic desire to have a relationship with Him; to come closer to Him, to worship Him, to adore and glorify Him.

 Unfailing Love by Chris Tomlin

Prayer: Father, You are so amazing. I want and need Your love so much. And though I am unworthy, though I don't show You my love as much as I should, You think I am truly someone special. Thank you. . . . .

Note to self

_____
_____
_____
_____
_____
_____
_____
_____
_____
_____
_____

Day 10

The Tortoise & The Hare

I'm sure you are familiar with the fable of the tortoise and the hare. The story relates the importance of a slow, steady pace until your goal is met. Likewise, your journey of prayer should start out slowly and develop as time goes along and as you gain or add more elements to your prayer. This is not a race to the end just for the sake of finishing. If that were so, you could easily read this book in a day or two. But the objective is to establish a routine or habit of daily time with God. So take your time, keep a steady pace, spend time daily with God knowing He is with you and He is truly proud of you for wanting to be more like Him!

Today, you are encouraged to pray for a brief fifteen minutes. Be honest with yourself and with God. If you set your standards too high in the amount of time you will spend in prayer, you are setting yourself up for failure; failure not only to yourself, but equally or more importantly, failure to God. If your prayer lasts longer than your set time (say, fifteen minutes) that is certainly okay, but remember the goal is to establish daily prayer. So, don't set your standards too high in the beginning. If your prayer time lasts less than fifteen minutes, that too is okay. Remember what is important, and that is to speak to God naturally, honestly until you have said what is on your mind.

As you begin your prayers, ask God to help you come closer to Him; that He might open your heart to hear His support and joy in you wanting to have this relationship with Him.

> Dear God, I want to take our relationship to a higher level. Help me in my prayers to You by. . . . .

There is no need to try to be the first to finish this "prayer race". Jesus tells His disciples the parable about the workers in the vineyard where those that worked only an hour were paid the same wage as those that worked all day. The last to be hired had waited all day in hopes of finding work; they persevered in their "race" to find work. In concluding the parable, Jesus said, "So the last will be first, and the first will be last" (Matthew 20.16).

The same is true for you in your "race". Set a good foundation of what prayer is about and the many different styles and formats you can use. Experiment, "test drive", find a comfortable format. Allow time for God to speak to you regarding the "road you are to race on". He will most certainly guide you along the right path. Then, when you reach the finish line (90 days) you will have won the race; you will have established a permanent and habitual relationship with Jesus Christ, Lord and Savior.

Note to self

_____
_____
_____
_____
_____
_____
_____
_____
_____
_____

Day 11

Statistics

A survey of U.S. adults and teenagers by Barna Research Ltd, from 1991-2001 revealed the following statistics about people's prayer habits:

Who Prays?
82% of adults and 89% of teenagers pray in a normal week.
88% of women and 75% of men pray in a typical week.
People living in the South and Midwest pray more than those living in the West and Northeast (around 86% to 76% respectively).
96% of born-again Christians pray weekly.

What do people pray about?
95% of people thank God for what He has done in their lives.
76% ask for forgiveness for specific sins.
67% worship God by praising His superior attributes.
61% ask for help for specific needs.
47% are silent during prayer to listen to God.

When and how much do people pray?
An average prayer lasts just under five minutes.
52% of people who pray do so several times a day.
37% of people say they pray once a day.

Data from the Pew Forum U.S. Religious Landscape Survey, conducted in 2007, among more than 35,000 Americans age 18 and older, discovered this:

The percent of those that prayed at least once per day by age groups:

18-29 = 48%
30-49 = 56%
50-64 = 61%
65+ = 68%

The percent of those that prayed at least once per day by income:

<$30,000 = 64%
$30,000-$49,999 = 59%
$50,000-$74,999 = 57%
$75,000-$99,999 = 52%
$100,000+ = 48%

An Ellis Research survey for Facts & Trends in 2005 finds just 16% of pastors are very satisfied with their personal prayer lives, 47% are somewhat satisfied, 30% somewhat dissatisfied, and 7% very dissatisfied. Their mean amount of prayer time per day is 30 minutes.

These numbers are interesting, but by no means should you place yourself in a category and plan your prayer life by that. I am just thankful you want to pray and are reading more about it in the hopes of coming closer to Christ!

Day _12_

The Praying Man

I n a book titled <u>Why Men Hate Going To Church</u>, Dr. Woody Davis discovered the number one response as to why men don't go to church is, "church is for women, children, and wimps."[43] In short, many men feel going to church threatens their masculinity. Sadly, I am afraid the same can be said about men and prayer. But hold on there pal, there may be a few "manly" men you have heard of that are notable Christian men who do pray: Drew Brees (NFL), Mariano Rivera (MLB), Jason Witten (NFL), Jake Peavy (MLB), Aaron Rogers (NFL), Michael Waltrip (NASCAR), Tony Dungy (NFL Coach), George Foreman (Boxer), Zach Johnson (PGA), and my favorite – Colt McCoy (NFL). And, a few others of interest like Kurt Warner, Joe Gibbs, Shawn Alexander, John Smoltz, Mike Singletary, Albert Pujols, and Tim Tebow. But let's not forget the most famous and important "celebrity" of them all – Jesus! Each of these men is man enough to openly profess their love of God, so what's your problem. . . . Man UP! And get on your knees.

It is man's business to pray, but it takes manly men to do it. It is godly business to pray, and it takes godly men to do it. And it is godly men who give themselves over entirely to God.[44]

"The prayer of a righteous man is powerful and effective" (James 5.16). Are you a praying man, ever praying that God would fashion you according to His will? Are you an example of holiness?[45]

All too often men say they are too busy to pray. You know, they have priorities like work, golf, fixing the car, too tired, the game is on television, yard work, and the list is only limited to your imagination. Few men lay themselves out in great prayer. The great business of praying is a hurried, petty, starved, beggarly business with most men.[46]

Until you feel free to be you in your relationship with God, it's not a real relationship.[47] So maybe today you should consider asking God to give you the strength and will power to be the man He made you to be; to be manly enough to stand up for your beliefs regardless of what the "boys" say; to have the courage to proudly profess your love of God to anyone.

Who tops your list of "favorite men"? Are they Christian men or are they men that are just good at what they do? Who are some of your favorite men "friends"? Are they Christians. . . or do they just play a good game of golf, or like the same football team as you do, or maybe they just drink a lot of beer.

List some of your favorite men and why

_____
_____
_____
_____
_____
_____
_____
_____
_____
_____
_____

Day 13

The Praying Woman

There are hundreds of examples of prayer in the Bible, most of which are by men, but they also apply to women. The Bible does not apply to just one gender; it applies to both men and women alike. It is not by coincidence that women play very critical parts in the Bible. Though not part of the well-known "twelve disciples", women were indeed disciples of Christ and are described in many stories of the Bible and parables of Jesus.

"In bitterness of soul Hannah wept much and prayed to the Lord. And she made a vow saying, 'O Lord Almighty, if you will only look upon your servant's misery and remember me, and not forget your servant but give her a son, then I will give him to the Lord for all the days of his life, and no razor will ever be used on his head'" (1 Samuel 1.10-11). Hannah's prayer was from the heart as she expressed her desires in the midst of bitterness, desperation, and weeping. The following two verses (1 Samuel 1.12-13) describe Hannah's prayer from her heart, yet no words were heard by Eli, the priest. He assumed Hannah was drunk and moving her lips with no sound. However Hannah assured Eli that she was not drunk, but was praying from extreme emotions of anguish and grief.

In Hannah's barren state and so wanting a child, she made a promise to the Lord that she would give the child to the Lord's service if only He would grant her a baby. God did His part. . . and the faithful servant Hannah did her part too. Samuel was born and spent his life serving God under the priest Eli. Hannah offered a prayer to God that became known as Hannah's Prayer.

Please refer to and read 1 Samuel 2.1-10. Have you ever been desperate? Are you desperate right now? Turn to God; talk to Him; He wants to hear from you.

"There was also a prophetess, Anna, the daughter of Phanuel, of the tribe of Asher. She was very old; she had lived with her husband seven years after her marriage, and then was a widow until she was eighty-four. She never left the temple but worshiped night and day, fasting and praying. She gave thanks to God and spoke about the child all were looking forward to as the redemption of Jerusalem" (Luke 2.36-38). What an inspiring woman! Anna had every right to be angry and to give up her praying after her husband of seven years died. Nevertheless, she never surrendered her hope of God sending a Savior to redeem the world.

I have personally known women who traveled to church every morning to pray to God and be in His presence. And, of course, I know many women that pray to God in their personal "sanctuary" in the comforts of their own home. Some of these women were very similar to Anna. . . old and widowed, yet full of confidence in the promise of God sending His Son to be our Savior. Do you have the faith of Anna in the hope of Jesus Christ as our Savior? Is there something holding you back from daily prayer with God? Tell Him about it. He's listening.

Judges 5.1-31 is a lengthy prayer by the judge of Israel, Deborah. Her prayer is a song that combines many components that may be applied to prayer today. It includes praise, exalting the Lord for His help. It confers blessing on Him and for people He used. At times it is an acclamation of tribute to God for His work and for people He used. And, it includes both intercessory and petitional prayer requests.[48]

Ladies, are you a woman of God? Do you praise Him, thank Him, pray to Him as often as you should. You have had far more influence in the Bible than you may know. . . and you certainly have tremendous influence on men of today. Gently lead, guide, encourage "your man" to a closer relationship with Christ. . . pray for him!

Lord God, thank you for the many women of the Bible that stood up and prayed so openly to you. Be with me as I now turn to you and pray. . . . .

Day 14

I'm Only a Kid

Okay, let's set the record straight. The dude writing this book is in his 60s. I know; it bums me out, too. But, the content of this devotional does not relate only to older folks. If you believe in God, if you believe Jesus Christ died and rose again for the forgiveness of your sins, then you should seek a closer relationship with Him regardless of your age.

Next, do not be upset with the title of this "day". You see, to me anyone younger than the age of 50 is a kid. (Someday you will be in my shoes, and it won't be so funny.) But specifically, in using the term "kid," I am targeting those younger people age 25 and below. Within that age bracket, I would like to break it down to two categories – elementary age kids and below, and middle school age and above.

Nowhere does the Bible say that young people should not pray or don't have to pray. Though we older folks often tend to "excuse" the youngsters from praying, the fact is the Bible implies that everyone should pray to God.

Those that are roughly under the age of 12 are in the early formative years of prayer. As a parent, your focus for these kids should be to establish the basic elements of prayer and encourage the formation of a less structured prayer life:

1. At the same time each day, make it a habit to talk to God.
2. In a quiet place (no television, social media, music, etc.) begin the conversation with God.

3. Make prayers of praise, petitions, requests, and confession. Keep it simple and let the children speak in a comfortable manner.
4. Begin the habit of reading Scripture. Read a verse a day and discuss what that verse implies and how it applies to life today.

For those older than 12 years of age, it's time to get more serious. You are old enough and mature enough to speak to God in a more grown up way. Any of the formats in this book will fit you. Just pray in the style that suits you. You are encouraged to pray in small groups (say 2 or 3 people of your age). The key thing is to begin a HABIT of prayer.

Young people that openly profess their faith in God and/or pray in public are a huge inspiration to me (and most other older folks). It makes my heart swell with pride to see our youth openly expressing their love of God and "their neighbor" for others. I sadly admit I personally was not that courageous during my younger years. I was very shy and felt insecure about my knowledge and awareness of God. Maybe you are not that knowledgeable either, but know that your tenacity and love of God are admirable. So here, here, I applaud you and can only say "Keep It Up"!

 You Rock!

As a "young Christian", you have a huge impact on other people; far more so than I do. Don't think for a minute that you don't have an influence on others. . . both young and old. Step up and be someone. Let your peers and the rest of us older folks know that you know who God is and are not afraid to let others know.

"Be strong and courageous" (Deuteronomy 31.6)!

Day __15__

Bearpaw Samples

Beginning Prayers

To prepare yourself for this time with God, you should first set an atmosphere of reverence and set your heart in a setting of holiness. You should begin with a time of silence (30-60 seconds), followed by an opening prayer or multiple prayers. Each person is different, and consequentially has different prayer needs, so there is no set prayer to begin with. In fact, you may find that changing your opening prayers from time to time is beneficial. Following are prayers I use to begin prayer time:

"Almighty and everlasting God, you are always more ready to hear than we to pray, and to give more than we either desire or deserve. Pour upon us the abundance of your mercy, forgiving us those things of which our conscience is afraid, and giving us those good things for which we are not worthy to ask."[49]

I personally follow this prayer with, "Almighty God, help me to remember what is really important; that I am Your child, and You are my Father (Abba). You love me for who I am and how I live, not for what I look like or what I own. Let me praise You who sees into my heart, yet still loves me and is always with me."

Lord, how can I worship You today?
(love, respect, praise, service, music, prayer, dancing, etc.)
How can I show my love for You and others today?
What words can I say that will honor and bless You?
What act of service can I do to represent Your love?
What song of praise can I sing that would please You?
What passage of Scripture are You calling me to read?
How would Your Spirit inspire me to pray today?
What is Your will for me, Lord?

These prayers are offered as ideas and samples only. If you like them, you are welcome to use them, or modify them to fit your needs. Spend a few minutes thinking about how you will prepare your mind and heart in preparation for prayer. Most likely the prayer you work out today will be changed, modified, or even totally replaced as time goes along – and that is really okay.

Make your prayers for the next few days very simple. Pray for your family – their needs, your wishes, and God's will. Pray for your friends, church family, co-workers, and others in your life. Pray for these people by name and specific needs they may have. Be honest with God, be open with Him, have faith that He hears you. Thank God for His presence with you, and tell Him you will talk to Him more as the day goes along and tomorrow unfolds.

Note to self

_____
_____
_____
_____
_____
_____
_____
_____
_____

Day 16

When to Pray

Jesus prayed at all times of the day—morning, noon, evening, and at night – so there is no right or wrong time to pray. The important thing for you to consider is to establish a time of day for prayer that fits your schedule. If you try to force a "time" that is not compatible to your schedule, you will ultimately give up and quit. So really pray about what time God wants you to visit Him, and make a commitment to stick with it. Remember, God is not asking for your ability, He's asking for your availability.[50] Later, when you have established the importance of prayer in your life and are committed to the sacrifice, then you may consider changing the time you have set. You will never have time for prayer, you must make time.[51]

Did you know. . . . .

Pious Jews of Jesus time prayed publicly at three set times of the day: morning (third hour, 9:00 am), evening (ninth hour, 3:00 pm), and at sunset.[52]

With all that being said, it seems that in the morning would be a good time to offer prayers. The men (and women) who have done the most for God in this world have been early on their knees. If God is not first in your thoughts and efforts in the morning, He will be in the last place the remainder of the day.[53]

King David sought God early, before daylight. "In the morning, O Lord, you hear my voice; in the morning I lay my requests before you and wait in expectation" (Psalm 5.3). You are the fittest for prayer when you are the freshest and not yet filled with the business of the day. Mornings are when we have most need of prayer, considering the dangers and temptations of the day ahead.[54] In the morning, your mind is more free from problems, and then you can commit the whole day to God. Regular communication helps any friendship and is certainly necessary for a strong relationship with God.[55]

"But I cry to you for help, O Lord; in the morning my prayer comes before you" (Psalm 88.13).

Philip Henry said, "Pray alone. Let prayer be the key of the morning and the bolt at night. The best way to fight against sin is to fight it on your knees.[56]

If you cannot pray in the morning, pray when you can! God is available 24 hours a day, seven days a week. . . 24/7!

Possibly you could pray during your break at work, during your lunch hour (take a walk, eat your sandwich [or fast], and pray for 20-30 minutes), sit in the park, or pray while you are commuting. In the evening, consider skipping a television show (designate a specific time each evening).

As a past Physical Education teacher, I dedicate the first two hours of my day (7:00 am – 9:00 am) to PE. . . . Prayer & Exercise!

APE: Always **P**ray **E**veryday

Make a covenant (commitment) with God for a **regular time** of prayer. This is your word to Him that you love Him enough to make this promise to Him.

Day 17

Where to Pray

Your personal prayers should be done in dedicated, undisturbed privacy, not to seek the attention of others, but to worship your God who waits for you there. This is your dedication of time to God in prayer. Private places and plenty of time are the life of prayer.[57] Find a place of focus; a loft, a garden, a spare room, an attic, even a designated chair – somewhere away from the routine hustle/bustle of life, out of the patch of distractions (phone, television, radio, doorbell, kids, dog, birds, people, traffic, even a ticking clock). Allow this spot to become a sacred "tent of meeting." "Now Moses used to take a tent and pitch it outside the camp some distance away, calling it the 'tent of meeting'" (Exodus 33.17). Tent of meeting is used some 140 times in the Old Testament to describe a special tent where the Israelites worshiped God – a place where God would meet His people.

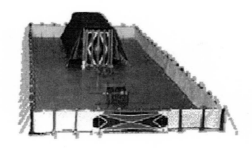

"When you pray, go into your room, close the door and pray to your Father, who is unseen" (Matthew 6.6). Some translations of the Bible call this room a closet or inner chamber. What will you call your "place of prayer". . . sanctuary, refuge, upper room, prayer room, meeting room? Regardless of what you call it, you need to visit it daily.

To help you have uninterrupted time with God, you might consider advising your family and friends of your prayer time and ask that they do not disturb you during that time unless it is an emergency.

Maybe you like change and spontaneity! Your place of prayer can be any place that offers you quietness, peace, and oneness with God:

Isaac went into the field. (Genesis 24.63)
Christ went to a mountain top. (Luke 6.12, Mark 6.46)
Peter went to a house top. (Acts 10.9)
Disciples went to an upper room. (Acts 1.13-14)
Cornelius prayed in the house of Mary. (Acts 12.5-17)
Paul and companions prayed by a river. (Acts 16.13)
Disciples prayed on a beach. (Acts 21.5)
Jesus prayed in a solitary place. (Mark 1.35, Luke 4.42)
Jesus prayed alone. (Luke 9.18)
Jesus prayed in the Garden of Gethsemane. (Mark 14.32-42)

Whether you gather in a cathedral, or a tiny congregation, or pray alone in a home chapel, the communion of saints gathers with you in your humble prayers of thanksgiving for the journey of Christ.[58]

At some point today, turn off your television, cell phone, tablet, radio and iPod, and simply listen for God's voice. Then quiet your extraneous thoughts, and focus on Him.

My Father God, I seek time alone with you. I truly want to come closer to you and feel I can do that best right now without distractions. Lead me to the place you would have me spend time with you. Take away my thoughts about everything that interferes with my worship of you. Provide for me as much time as You need for us to spend quality time together. Amen.

Day 18

Humility

"For everyone who exalts himself will be humbled, and he who humbles himself will be exalted" (Luke 18.14). Think about this passage for a minute or so.

Each person, being human, has the innate desire to create and fulfill our own destiny – our own status, wealth, and even final outcome of our life. You may be like many who still try to buy or earn your rewards from God. You may still have the mind-set that YOU can make it all happen. Well, you can't. You know that all things come from God, so make it a habit right now to humble yourself to a greater power.

Humility does not have its eyes on self, but rather on God and others. It is willing to take the lowliest seat and prefers those places where it will be unnoticed. In humility there is a total absence of pride. It does not seek publicity, nor hunt for high places.[59] An excellent example of humility is from the parable of Jesus at the wedding feast (Luke 14.7-14).

Humility is an indispensable requisite of true prayer. Prayer has no beginning, no ending, and no being, without humility.[60] For neither pride nor vanity can pray.[61] The self-ward soul runs around saying "I am doing my best for the glory of God." The God-ward soul can relax and proclaim, "God is doing His wonderful work in the wreck that is me."[62]

> J.O.Y.
>
> **J**esus first. **O**thers second. **Y**ourself last.

To respect God's majesty, you must compare yourself to His greatness. When you look at creation, you often feel small by comparison. This is a healthy way to get back to reality, but God does not want you to dwell on your smallness. Humility means proper respect for God, not self-depreciation.[63]

Take a look at your prayer life and ask God to reveal any areas driven by pride as you say, THE LITANY OF HUMILITY[64]:

O Jesus! Meek and humble of heart, hear me
From the desire of being esteemed, deliver me, Jesus;
From the desire of being loved. . .
From the desire of being extolled. . .
From the desire of being honored. . .
From the desire of being praised. . .
From the desire of being preferred to others. . .
From the desire of being consulted. . .
From the desire of being approved. . .
From the fear of being humiliated. . .
From the fear of being despised. . .
From the fear of suffering rebukes. . .
From the fear of being forgotten. . .
From the fear of being ridiculed. . .
From the fear of being wronged. . .
From the fear of being suspected. . .
That others may be loved more than I
Jesus, grant me the grace to desire it.
That others may be esteemed more than I. . .
That, in the opinion of the world,
others may increase and I may decrease. . .
that others may be chosen and I set aside. . .
that others may be praised and I unnoticed. . .
that others may be preferred to me in everything. . .
that others may become holier than I, provided that I may become as holy as I should.

Day 19

How to Pray

F irst and foremost, God's priority in prayer is not so much how you pray but more so in what you pray about and the attitude of your heart while you pray. Everyone's experience with God and with prayer is unique, there is no ONE way to talk to God. It is not important how your friends pray or how long they pray. You do not need to follow every detail of this book just because it works for me or someone else. However, it is certainly alright to use ideas and concepts from others if it improves your relationship with God. There are many old adages you can think of such as: "You don't need to reinvent the wheel;" and "If it isn't broken, don't fix it." So understand fully there really is no right or wrong way to pray, but as time goes along you will discover some "styles" or "formats" fit your needs better than others.

Ultimately, your primary goal in prayer is to know the will of God.[65] We will talk more about this in a few days. You can pray out loud or silently - standing, sitting, kneeling, or lying on the floor - eyes open or eyes closed - hands clasped, folded, high in the air, or out to your side. It really doesn't matter your "professional" level of speech. God understand your every thought and word. So just be you – be honest, be sincere, be you! True praying is not mere eloquent speech. Remember that Moses stuttered (Exodus 4.10). Speech from the heart, followed by the constant doing of God's will in your daily life, that is what gives prayer potency.[66] In fact, desperate prayers are one of the clearest ways for you to honor God. Saying "Lord, I need you," acknowledges His importance to you. He is essential, after all, and the desperate soul is not afraid to say so.[67]

It is alright to be human. God knows your weakness as a human, and understands you will have moments of failure in your prayer life. There will be times when you simply do not want to pray. Even if your desire to pray is absent, your judgment tells you that you ought to pray. In such circumstances, you should pray for the "desire to pray."[68]

At the same time, your mind will eventually wander to far off places while you are praying. Don't be surprised or upset; just know it will happen. God understands. . . . Simply return your attention back to Him and continue praying.[69] Lack of focus is one of the reasons for choosing a place of prayer away from as many distractions as possible. Hearing the radio or the television is an easy source to draw you away from your thoughts, meditations, and conversation with God. You will most likely never be able to totally eliminate all distractions, so just be prepared at some time to RE-FOCUS.

Remember this. . . . .
The most important aspect of prayer is to be yourself.

Today – what are your family needs? Pray for them by name. Are there prayers that have been answered or things you are thankful in your life? Thank God for His unending love, mercy, and care. Be sure to set your appointment with God for tomorrow, and don't be late!

Note to self

_____

_____

_____

_____

_____

_____

_____

_____

_____

Day 20

Talk to Me, Johnny

In the movie "Rambo: First Blood", Colonel Trautman is communicating via walkie talkie with Vietnam veteran John Rambo. The Colonel desperately says, "Talk to me, Johnny" in a plea for Rambo to talk to him. Eventually Rambo does talk to the Colonel. . . emotionally telling him why he is in such a state of turmoil.

Can you guess where this is going? Sure, you know God is making the same plea to you. . . "talk to me". . .He is saying He wants to have a conversation with you. He is openly and proudly saying He loves you and wants the relationship with you to go to the next level!

Clement of Alexandria, a third-century philosopher from Egypt said, "Prayer is conversation with God." This means we talk to God, it is not just wishing and hoping. We express our thoughts, feelings, dreams, feelings, hopes, and fears to God.[70]

Be yourself; simple prayer is the most common form of prayer in the Bible. Simply and unpretentiously share your concerns and petitions. This involves ordinary people bringing ordinary requests to a loving and compassionate Father.[71] There is no need for fancy words, eloquent speeches, or lengthy oracles. Talk to God just like you would your friend. Prayer is so simple; it is nothing more than talking to God. . . and listening to what He has to say."[72] "For your Father knows what you need before you ask Him" (Matthew 6.8). He is not waiting to be informed of your needs. He knows your every thought and prayer before you ask. It is not what you say, or don't say; it is the fact you are seeking Him and communicating with Him. He seeks your relationship and communication with Him to express your dependence on Him and your faith and trust in His answer to you. Prayer is the expression of the human heart in conversation with God. . . it is a dialogue between two persons who love each other.[73] Prayer is the direct result of relationship with Christ. Without relationship, prayer becomes mere performance.[74]

Like Hannah (1 Samuel 1.9-11), you may sometimes find it difficult to form the proper words for prayer. But God hears your heart's cry even when your mouth is silent.[75] Most likely you are not a professional speaker, so don't try to pretend to be one. (If however, you ARE a professional speaker, good for you, speak up; but remember prayer is what comes from the heart, not the mouth.)

Talk to me. . . . .

Think about this:

Prayer is not just an activity, or ritual, or an obligation. Nor is it begging God to do what you want Him to do. It is communion and communication with God that touches His heart.[76]

From Psalm 139:

O Lord, you have examined my heart and know everything about me; today I ask. . . . .

Note to self

_____
_____
_____
_____
_____
_____
_____
_____
_____
_____
_____

Day 21

Who Am I?

You are you. You are not me. You are probably not a pastor, a celebrity, or anyone famous. You are not 16th century "thee and thou". You are you! God made you as a unique being, and He loves what He made. So, when you go to Him in prayer you don't need to pretend to be someone else; be **YOU**!

You must be honest and sincere when talking to God. He wants to hear from you, not someone that you are not. Jesus said, "Do not be like the hypocrites" (Matthew 6.5). [We will talk about the Pharisees later in the book] Trying to convince God you are someone you are not simply will not work. King David tells you in Psalm 139 that God knows you better than you know yourself. He says, "O Lord, you have searched me and you know me" (Psalm 139.1). The Psalm goes on for 24 verses exclaiming how God knows you so very well. He should; after all, He is the one that who created you!

If you are being honest, you will openly admit you are a sinner and desperately need God's mercy and grace. And if you are like most people, your ultimate goal is to spend eternity with God in heaven. So accept the fact you are not perfect—in fact, far from it. But also accept the fact God will meet you more than half-way if you give yourself to Him – give yourself to Him – give YOU to Him. He wants you, just as you are, to come to Him every day and talk to Him. One of my favorite lines in The Shack is, "God is especially fond of you."[77] You are so special to Him, especially when you approach Him as you. He knows you as the person He made and expects you to come to Him as He made you. . . honest and sincere. . . as you!

The Bible makes many references to the joy of marriage. The picture of God's love is often that of a husband's love for the woman of his dreams; an emotional, sky-high feeling; exhilarating, almost "giddy." The groom marries his wonderful bride for better or for worse, for richer or for poorer. This is exactly how God accepts you; He is your ultimate partner in life! "As a young man marries a maiden, so will your sons marry you; as a bridegroom rejoices over his bride, so will your God rejoice over you" (Isaiah 62.5). This image is a painting of God's unending, unconditional, fathomless love for you. It is much like our entry into heaven will be; so overwhelming that we simply cannot understand or comprehend it. It is so much more than we could ever imagine. That is how much God loves you *right now*. Regardless of what you have done; no matter how inadequate you may feel, the heart of God is over-flowing with love for you. So you see, you don't need to be someone else – someone you are not. God knows who you are and He love that person. Be thankful He made you who you are and how you are. . . be **YOU**!

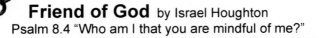

Friend of God by Israel Houghton
Psalm 8.4 "Who am I that you are mindful of me?"

Day 22

What to Pray For

The things and people you pray for will of course vary from time to time. A person in need today very well may be a person of thanksgiving tomorrow. Your prayer requests will change from day to day just as the needs of the world change from day to day. Following are a number of common things and people that are often included in personal prayers:

People – husband, wife, kids, parents, close friends, co-workers, pastor, church family, those in other religious faiths, atheists.

Reasons for prayer – for those struggling with addiction, love, marriage, worry, stress, abuse, family relationships, relationship with God. Those in need of healing, seeking a job, financial stability, seeking to find God.

America – our president, law makers, state and local governments, economic failure of USA & the world, safety of our military, disasters & tragedies.

World affairs – politics, poverty, spread of the Gospel, church persecutions, peace among nations.

Pray for your children's purity, passion for Christ, discernment, faith, hope, love, and for their school.

Pray for yourself – for your career, for forgiveness of sins, guidance, wisdom to make good decisions, world and community service.

For ALL – that each will come closer to Christ every day.

Thanksgiving – you could spend hours in this category.

And finally, a prayer my wife says daily, "Pray for those that have no one to pray for them."

Prayer is approaching God in order to ask Him to accomplish His will on earth.[78] Are you truly communicating with God or just asking Him for favors? Give God all your weaknesses: physical, emotional, and spiritual.[79] Nothing is too small for God's love, and nothing is too great for God's power. If it is big enough to cause you anxiety, it is big enough to take to the Lord in prayer.[80]

I struggle with a constant awareness of God's presence with me. So much in fact, that I have a short prayer I say often to remind me of His presence with me (you will see it later). The first Book of the Bible assures us of God's continual presence with us, "I am with you and will watch over you wherever you go" (Genesis 28.15). So, assuming you are a believer in Christ, when you enter into prayer you do not need to ask God to be with you. . . He is there! Instead, pray that you will be aware of His presence.

 He Knows My Name by Tommy Walker

Know this. . . . .

Jesus knows exactly what this day holds for you. He will not show you what is on the road ahead, but He will thoroughly equip you for the journey. Be willing to follow where He leads.[81]

There is one more thing of vital importance to pray for. We will talk about that tomorrow. Happy praying!

Day 23

God's Will

"When you ask, you do not receive, because you ask with wrong motives, that you may spend what you get on your pleasures" (James 4.3). Asking with wrong motives is a disgrace and dishonor to God. Wrong motives are seeking things of this world (such as clothes, a "status" car, or a higher paying job so you can have more things), and thus gratify your own pride and vanity instead of seeking to honor and glorify God.[82]

If you ask for things that are contrary to the will of God, you will be frustrated. Jesus always prayed for God's will to be done, then He worked to accomplish it.[83] "This is the confidence we have in approaching God: that if we ask anything according to His will, He hears us" (1 John 5.14). The Lord Christ encourages you to come to God in all circumstances, with all your supplications and requests. Through Him your petitions are admitted and accepted by God. The matter of your prayer must be in agreement with the declared will of God. It is not fit that you should ask what is contrary either to His majesty and glory or for your own good.

Whether you are praying for yourself, family, community, national, or world needs, you must seek to be in agreement with God's will so His purposes can reign on the earth.[84]

Two of the most inspirational statements of surrender and giving one's self to God are found in the gospel of Luke:

Jesus said, "Not my will, but yours be done" (Luke 22.42).

"I am the Lord's servant," Mary answered. "Let it be to me as you have said" (Luke 1.38).

"If you remain in me and my words remain in you, ask whatever you wish, and it will be given you" (John 15.7). There are two conditions to answered prayer; to remain in Jesus and for His words to remain in you. To remain or abide in Jesus is to commune with Him through worship, fellowship, and praying with Him. Secondly, are His words living in you? A good test is the first thing that comes out of your mouth when something goes wrong. Is it your faith boldly coming forth or is it frustration, anger, fear, or doubt?[85]

Pray today again for your family, friends, and needs. This time really focus on truly seeking God's will instead of just wishing and hoping something good will happen for these people. Tomorrow we will spend more time talking about and defining God's will and how to apply it to your prayer.

God Will Make A Way by Don Moen

Heavenly Father, You have said, "Many are the plans in a man's heart, but it is the Lord's purpose that prevails" (Proverbs 19.21). I ask You to fulfill Your word and make Your purpose reign in my life. Align my plans and goals with Your plans, and take away whatever is not from You. Renew my mind so I may understand Your ways and Your plans more fully. I pray this in the name of Jesus, who is my Way, Truth, and Life. Amen.[86]

Day 24

What Is God's Will?

The first rule of prayer is not "faith", but whether the request is according to God's will.[87] Real prayer is not simply asking God to bless what you have decided to do. It is coming to Him with an open mind and heart and inviting Him to plant His desires within you.[88]

How will you know what God's will is? By listening to – knowing – His Word! Carefully studying the Bible reveals the Lord's will and purpose for you. You discover God's will by reading and studying His word, by hiding it in your heart, and by letting the Word dwell in you richly.[89]

When you call to God for help, consider your motive. Is it to save yourself pain and embarrassment or to bring God glory and honor?[90] Some simple questions to ask yourself before bringing a request to the Lord are: "If God granted this request. . . . ."

Would it bring glory to Him?
Would it advance His kingdom?
Would it help others?
Would it help me grow spiritually?
Does it contradict what the Bible says?

Knowing and discerning God's will is sometimes difficult. Most of us want God to give us a direct, concise, specific answer – but that rarely happens. When God wants us to wait a while before granting an answer, we sometimes consider His answer to be no.

Or, sometimes His answer is no but we don't hear that and assume He is wanting us to wait longer for His answer. God wants us to make choices that are in agreement with His will. God will place His desires on your heart if only you will listen. The key is wanting God's will and not your own. If you truly seek God's will with a humble spirit and an open mind, He will reveal His will to you.

"For my Father's will is that everyone who looks to the Son and believes in him shall have eternal life" (John 6.40).

"It is God's will that you should be sanctified" (1 Thessalonians 4.3).

"Be joyful always; pray continually; give thanks in all circumstances, for this is God's will for you in Christ Jesus" (1 Thessalonians 5.16-18).

"For it is God's will that by doing good you should silence the ignorant talk of foolish men" (1 Peter 2.15).

As you pray today, ask yourself if your requests are your wishes or your true feelings for what God wants. Be honest; God knows what is in your heart.

At some point today, turn off your televison, radio, cell phone, tablet, and iPad, and simply listen to the gentle voice of God. Ask Him to reveal His will for you today and the days to come.

My Dear Father,

Open my heart to an intimate relationship with you every day and to following Your thoughts instead of my own, or those of others. . . . . .

Day 25

Pray for Who?

L et's start with you! See if you are anywhere in this scenario.
      "I don't like worshiping in church. Those people are hypocrites!"

Or, during your day have you ever encountered a gossipy co-worker, a mouthy teen-ager (or adult), a driver cutting in front of you, a boss who won't listen, a know-it-all, a loud, obnoxious drunkard in a restaurant, or someone that has done you wrong? The list could go on and on.

Have you ever thought that the **one** that needs prayer the most is you? Jesus shed His blood on the cross for all because of His unending love. He loves those "obnoxious" people just as much as He loves you.

KEEP THIS IN MIND: you will be spending an eternity. . . ETERNITY (that is a l-o-n-g, long time). . . in heaven with these same people worshiping our loving God. You will be singing praises to God with them every day. And you will love these people that you are having difficulties with today just as much as God loves them. Maybe you should consider starting to love them more today (just saying)!

Lord Jesus, how selfish and self-centered I am! Open my
heart to be more like you. Help me. . . . .

But I don't like the President. My stance on birth control is different. She really hurt my feelings. But, he's not a Christian. No way, he is so arrogant. What a wicked witch! DO YOU KNOW HOW LONG ETERNITY IS?

When God places difficult people in your life, don't simply discount them and walk away, but seek the Father and learn from Him why they have been brought into your life. When you receive God's perspective through prayer, it will change the way you relate to them.[91]

Remember that Jesus came into the world as a human and experienced everything you do today. His example of love is our model and commandment to follow in our lives. He, too, had those in His life that were "less than ideal," yet He loved them equally as much as any other. Jesus encountered the Samaritan woman at the well (John 4), a man with leprosy (Matthew 8.2), meals with sinners (Luke 15.2), the blind, lame, lepers, deaf, poor, and dead (Matthew 11.5), an adulterous woman (John 8), and a tax collector (Matthew 9.9). But Paul reminds us, "There is neither Jew nor Greek, slave nor free, male nor female, for you are all one in Christ Jesus" (Galatians 3.28). Have you prayed for something good to happen to those on your "outcast" list today?

H.O.P.E.

He Offers Peace Everyday

Consider this. . . . .

Sit quietly before the Lord and ask Him to lay a specific person on your heart and mind. Ask God how to pray for this person, to lead you in prayer on his or her behalf.[92]

Day 26

Bearpaw Samples

Prayer Lists

You may find it helpful to keep a list of your prayer concerns. Those of us that are older often find it difficult to remember all those we wish to pray for each day. I personally am accused of being "very organized" by my friends. I think that may be a polite way of saying I have Obsessive Compulsive Disorder. So it would be no surprise to those that know me that I keep a journal/ledger of my prayer requests.

There are many commercial prayer notebooks on the market for your review and purchase. However, to find one that totally fits your needs may be difficult, as we are all different.

A good option for your consideration is to create your own prayer notebook. . . which may also serve as a prayer journal (more on that in Day 73). The prayer ledger I use is a common 6" X 8" journal found in most any Christian Book Store, even many retail stores. It is a Book-like ledger with 150 or so lined pages where one may write their own text, creating an individualized style of notebook. I update my prayer list each month to a new page, adding new prayer requests, moving some requests to "thanksgiving", and deleting some requests. I have used the same "journal" for the past six years and still have at least three years' worth of pages left. A normal binder that requires the insertion of regular lined school book would also be an easy adaptation for your prayer notebook.

Sample Page of Bearpaw's Prayer List

January 2014

Pray for Imamediate Family:
    Wife, son, me

Pray for Family:
    Parents, siblings, in-laws, any in need, God-daughter

Pray for God's Grace & Love:
    Neighbors, priest/pastor, close friends

Pray for Healing:
    List all you feel the call to pray for.

Pray for Those Affected by Disaster or Tragedy:
    Victims of hurricanes, floods, earthquakes, tornadoes, shootings, wildfires, and other tragedies.

Pray for Those in Need of Work:
    Pray for all in need.

Pray for Those in Need of Love or Reconciliation:
    List the names of those you will pray for.

Pray for God's Presence in Time of Need:
    For any that have the need for His presence, such as America, drought areas, bible study group, church, the spread of His Word, church prayer list, etc.

(From my wife: for those who have no one to pray for them.)

Others:

Day 27

So Many to Pray For!

I t is easy for any and all of us to fall into a prayer rut. Eventually you may find that you pray for the same things day after day, almost in rote fashion: your spouse, your family, your friends, your co-workers, and those in need of healing. All of these are admirable but how often (if ever) do you pray for the "lost", those who are persecuted for praying to God in public, those living in the poorest countries that have never heard the Word of God, those devastated by disasters around the world, the missionaries caring for and spreading hope of Jesus to others, or. . . .?

Ask the Lord to show you the people, situations, and ministries He wants you to pray for. You may find that as your prayer life evolves and grows, you discover you are praying for things and people you may not have expected to. You may, in fact, have such a large prayer list that you pray for certain things or people on a certain day of the week. There is truly an unending list of topics, areas, things, and people to pray for and you cannot pray for everything.[93] If your prayer list gets so long (and I hope it does) that you have to categorize or departmentalize the list, there are logical ways to do this (but again, no rules). So let's take a look at some topics and an approach to pray for the so many in need:

Not considering the numerous suggestions in the next days, the following is a model of prayer for your consideration. Of course, the topic or areas of prayer could be adapted to fit your own personal needs.

Day of Week	Topic / Area of Prayer
Monday	**The World**: Disasters, peace, economy, health or illness, governments, food, rain for drinking and crops, the spread of the Good News, missionaries, orphanages
Tuesday	**Friends**: God's presence, acceptance of Jesus as Savior, health, jobs
Wednesday	**The United States**: Our President, our law-makers, the economy, jobs, the homeless and needy, the hungry, safety of our military, those recovering from disaster or tragedy, the ill and those in need of better health, current activities of the week
Thursday	**Your Family**: Spouse, children, parents, grandparents, aunts & uncles, cousins, any family in need of prayer
Friday	**Thanksgiving**: Everyone has reasons to be thankful. Thank God for all He has blessed you with.
Saturday	**YOU**: What are your needs?
Sunday	**Corporate Prayer at Church**

Father, sometimes I get so self-centered that I fail to pray for my brothers and sisters outside of my family. Let me not forget the millions of others in the world that need to know of Your unending love and grace.

Day 28

Supplications

Supplication means to ask with earnestness, intensity, and per-severance.[94] Supplication is a common prayer word. In short, it means asking God for help. The Bible indicates there are two types of prayer—requests made to God and sincere thanksgiving or praise. "Do not be anxious about anything; but in everything, by prayer and petition (some translations say 'supplications'), with thanksgiving, present your requests to God" (Philippians 4.6). Many people simply regard both of the terms of prayer and peti-tions (supplications) with no difference between them, but actually there is a difference. So, what is the difference between prayer and petitions (supplications)?

I am going to focus on the word 'supplication' rather than petition. Supplication is a form of prayer in which you make heartfelt requests to God – you are asking for, pleading for, or requesting something from God. Generally, supplication is defined by petitions (asking for yourself) and intercessions (asking for others). You will find that many of your prayers fit into one of the supplication categories. Much of your prayer time will be spent in supplication. In the days to come, we will discuss a variety of means by which you can approach your supplications. Some may fit your style, others may not.

Prayer in general, keeping in mind Philippians 4.6, can of course include your requests to God but can also include prayers of thanksgiving, blessings, praise, etc. In supplications there is always a request, but not so in general prayers. A good example is you may pray saying 'bless my family', 'thank you for my new job', or 'You are such a loving and caring God'. But when you cry out to God for the cure of your wife's cancer or healing for a sick friend, you are making a supplication. In prayer you may praise the power and qualities of God. But this is not the case in supplication. Supplication entails only requests to God. Supplications are any requests made to God while prayer is any communication with God.

I think it is important to have knowledge of the difference in supplications, petitions, intercessions, and prayer in general, but not to the point of being fearful of "doing the right thing." Remember this—prayer that comes honestly from your heart IS "the right thing."

Precious Lord,

I may not ever understand all the terms and complexities of this simple yet difficult task I am taking on. Remind me of what is really important; that I am Your child and You are my Father. Let me not get bogged down in the intricate details of prayer. Help me focus only on what is genuine conversation from me to You. As I mature in my prayer life, then may I come to understand more fully the details of this great opportunity You have given me.

Note to self

_____
_____
_____
_____
_____
_____
_____
_____
_____

Day 29

Petitions

P etitions are the requests to God for <u>yourself</u>, you are asking God to help YOU. This is when we bring our daily needs and desires to our heavenly Father.[95] It is certainly acceptable and good to ask God for personal help, but remember this is only one aspect of your prayer life and requests.

You must remember to be realistic and honest in your requests. Ask yourself if your request is what God wants for you (is really His will). Jesus said, "Ask and it will be given to you" (Matthew 7.7). R-E-A-L-L-Y, do you think He meant, "Let me win the power ball drawing," or "Let the Cowboys win this game." You know your relationship with God is drawing closer when the requests for yourself evolve to meeting His will rather than your will.

Three Steps to Powerful Prayers of Petition (from sharp-church.org):

A. Regularly pray through each **fruit of the Holy Spirit** and ask God to develop the image and holiness of Christ within you. Gal 5.22-23 With each fruit you will not only ask God to fill you with that trait, but will also ask God to reveal how you are not living that particular fruit.

1. Prayers for Love
    a. A deep love for God. Romans 5:5
    b. A passionate and not a lukewarm love. Revelations 3:15
    c. A powerful love for things that will further His kingdom. Mt 6:33

70

d.   A love for souls and a passion to grow our church.

e.   A burning love for service.

f.   A love for family, friends, and enemies.

2. Joy

   a.   Filled with supernatural joy. 1 Peter 1:8

   b.   Teach me to rejoice and give praise. Philippians 4:4

3. Peace

   a.   Fill me with Your peace. Philippians 4:6-8

   b.   Teach me how not to worry.

4. Patience

   a.   Give me the ability to wait on you.

   b.   Allow me to endure without being impatient or complaining.

5. Kindness

   a.   Give me a kind and gracious attitude toward others.

   b.   Show me where I have been harsh or unkind to others.

6. Goodness

   a.   Give me a generous attitude toward others.

   b.   Show me how I have been selfish.

7. Faithfulness

   a.   Give me mountain-moving faith.

   b.   Show me how I have doubted you.

8. Gentleness

   a.   Fill me with a genuine humility, brokenness, and a repentant obedient spirit.

   b.   Reveal to me where I have been proud.

9. Self-control

   a.   Fill me with self-control and discipline.

   b.   Show me areas where I have been undisciplined, careless, or indulgent.

B. Regularly pray through the **Beatitudes** and ask God to conform you to these God characteristics. Matthew 5:1-10

1. Poor in spirit 2. Mournful 3. Meek 4. Need for righteousness 5. Merciful 6. Pure in heart 7. Peacemakers 8. Persecuted.

C. Regularly pray through other **character words** that are found in Scripture.

1. The anointing, power, and filling of the Holy Spirit 2. Spiritual passion (zeal) 3. Wisdom and discernment 4. A spirit of genuine worship 5. Protection from sins, self, Satan, and the world 6. The armor of God Ephesians 5:10-18

Day _30_

One Month!

Let's review some thoughts.

€   By now you should have an established time and place for your private time with God.
€   Do your family and friends know about your wishes not to be interrupted during your prayer time unless it is an emergency?
€   Are you reading from your Bible each day?
€   Are you seeking God's will?
€   Are there hindrances in your life that prevent you from coming closer to Christ – faults, sins, thoughts, un-forgiveness?
€   Are you keeping your word? Are you keeping your Day 1 covenant with God to pray every day? If you are, congratulations, keep it up! If you are not keeping your word with Him, how do you think that makes Him feel?

"I will remember my covenant. . ." (Gen 9.15)

There are still 60 days of this prayer devotional. There is a lot yet to be discussed and considered. For now, your daily prayer time should look something like this:

- € A quiet place to meet with God each day.
- € Assure there are no interruptions as you prepare to talk to God.
- € Have a "prayer log" of who and what you intend to pray for.
- € Begin with a time of silence to prepare your heart for this holy meeting.
- € Have beginning prayer (s).
- € Have your Bible handy.
- € Allow more time to pray than you first thought.
- € For now, pray primarily petitions and intercessions (we will add a lot more to this in the following month).
- € Close your time with a simple "thank you" and ending prayer.

 Everything Cries Holy by Robin Mark

Father, I simply ask that
You give me strength to continue.

Day 31

Intercessions

To pray for <u>others</u> is to intercede for them – to meditate or to stand in for another.[96] This obviously would include your family, friends, church family, co-workers, others in America, and even those in other countries you do not know. Samuel said, "Far be it from me that I should sin against the Lord by failing to pray for you" (1 Samuel 12.23). James, the half-brother of Jesus said, "Pray for each other" (James 5.16). The author of Hebrews said, "Therefore He (Jesus) is able to save completely those who come to God through Him, because He always lives to intercede for them" (Hebrews 7.25). The following is only a partial list of those for whom we are to offer intercessory prayers: all in authority (1 Timothy 2:2); ministers (Philippians 1:19); the church (Psalm 122:6); friends (Job 42:8); fellow countrymen (Romans 10:1); the sick (James 5:14); enemies (Jeremiah 29:7); those who persecute us (Matthew 5:44); those who forsake us (2 Timothy 4:16); and all men (1 Timothy 2:1).

When you pray for others you often do not know all the details or needs of the person in need. Don't worry; God knows every detail of that person and what he or she needs. The fact that you care enough about the person and seek God's will for them pleases God immensely. "We do not know what we ought to pray for, but the Spirit himself intercedes for us" (Romans 8.26). As you pray for others around the world, you are beginning to take the focus off of YOU, and you are giving your selfishness to God. Not only will those you are praying for be blessed, but you also will fill an inner need to help others by offering the greatest gift you have to give – PRAYER!

How to pray for other Christians.[97]

1. Be thankful for their faith and changed lives.
2. Ask God to help them know what He wants them to do.
3. Ask God to give them deep, spiritual understanding.
4. Ask God to help them live for Him.
5. Ask God to give them more knowledge of Himself.
6. Ask God to give them strength for endurance.
7. Ask God to fill them with joy, strength, and thankfulness.

A well-known parable about intercession from the Gospel of Luke says, "Suppose one of you has a friend, and he goes to him at midnight and says, 'Friend, lend me three loaves of bread, because a friend of mine on a journey has come to me, and I have nothing to set before him.' Then the one inside answers, 'Don't bother me. The door is already locked, and my children are with me in bed. I can't get up and give you anything.' I tell you, though he will not get up and give him the bread because he is his friend, yet because of the man's boldness he will get up and give him as much as he needs" (Luke 11.3-8).

A man has a friend come by his house late at night seeking help. He loved his friend and wanted to supply his friend's need, but had nothing to give. So he goes to the house of a rich friend and seeks help only to find none. But his perseverance in seeking help prevails and he is finally given what he asks for.

Day 32

I'll Be Praying for You

How many times have you said to a family member or friend, "I'll be praying for you" when you have discovered they have lost a loved one, or become ill, or have been in an accident, or lost their job, or. . . .?

Intercessory prayers for others are both powerful for the one being prayed for and for you. Indeed, the greatest gift anyone can give to God or to man is prayer. Prayer is a gift of love, and many that receive your prayers and later find out about them become very emotional. That is how powerful prayer is. Many are just overwhelmed someone else could love them enough to take time out of their day to pray for them.

As you express your love and concern for others, you exhibit your faith and belief in prayer to others as well as to God. You are also complying to God's command, "I urge then, first of all, that requests, prayers, intercession and thanksgiving be made for everyone" (1 Timothy 2.1).

But beware. . . . When you say "I will pray for you", you need to keep your word – not only to your friend, but to God as well (Yes, He heard you say it, too). This is another covenant you are making with God. If you don't really intend to pray for the person, don't say you will. Answer this question honestly:

"Do I keep my word when I tell someone I will pray for them?"

Did You Know

God made lots of covenants with his people and nations, and He kept His promise with every one of them. Here are the 5 great Bible covenants God made with man:

1. God's covenant with Noah Gen 9.17
2. God's covenant with Abraham Gen 12.1-3
3. God's covenant with Moses Ex 19.5-6
4. God's covenant with David 2 Sam 7.12-13
5. The covenant of Christ Luke 22.20

So, you tell someone you will pray for them after you have discovered a need of some kind. Very good, but have you ever considered saying these five powerful words to someone:

CAN I PRAY FOR YOU?

Instead of waiting to pray when you get home or are alone, consider offering a prayer on the spot – live, in person!

Can I Pray for You by Mark Bishop
http://www.youtube.com/watch?v=SkS3SQo2fhU

Prayer: Father, give me the strength and courage to help others in need by boldly asking if I can pray for them. I know this honors You, and at the same time offers comfort and hope to those being prayed for. May your loving light shine through my life to light the way for others as I offer prayers to them in Your name.

Note to self

Day 33

Healing

P raying for the sick, the injured, or any in need of any kind of healing is one of the most meaningful forms of prayer you can do. As you pray for God's will for a person in need, you are expressing your care and your love for them. . . and that pleases God! Jesus told the Pharisee expert in the law, "Love the Lord you God with all your heart and with all your soul and with all your mind. This is the first and greatest commandment. And the second is like it: 'Love your neighbor as yourself.' All the law and the prophets hang on these two commandments" (Matthew 22.37-40).

Nothing is beyond God's power, but you cannot guarantee that God will heal a particular person in the manner you want the person healed. What you can pray for any sick person is that God will bless them, and if it is His will, He will heal them.[98]

Healing of a person, including yourself, is not based on the quality of their faith (or yours), but on the power of our Lord who heals. You need only have faith that God knows the plans He has for this person (Jeremiah 29.11) and His will is being done (Luke 22.42).

Sometimes people ask, "What is the best way to pray for others?" Sri Daya Mata has said: "To pray for others is right and good. . .asking, above all, that they may be receptive to God, and thus receive physical, mental, or spiritual help direct from the Divine Physician. This is the basis of all prayer. God's blessing is ever present; receptivity is often lacking. Prayer heightens receptivity. . . .

"When you are affirming healing for others or yourself, visualize the tremendous force of God's healing power as a white light surrounding you or the person for whom you are praying. Feel that it is melting away all illness and imperfection. Every uplifting thought we think, every prayer we utter, every good action we perform, is impregnated with God's power. We can manifest this power in greater and greater ways as our faith becomes stronger and our love for God becomes deeper."

Following are two prayers taken from the internet.

Renew My Mind, Body and Soul

Lord, I come before you today in need of your healing hand. In you all things are possible. Hold my heart within yours, and renew my mind, body, and soul.

I am lost, but I am singing. You gave us life, and you also give us the gift of infinite joy. Give me the strength to move forward on the path you've laid out for me. Guide me towards better health, and give me the wisdom to identify those you've placed around me to help me get better.

In your name I pray, Amen.

To Heal a Friend

Think, o God, of our friend who is ill, whom we now commend to Your compassionate regard.

Comfort him upon his sickbed, and ease his suffering. We beg for deliverance, and submit that no healing is too hard for the Lord, if it be His will.

We therefore pray that You bless our friend with Your loving care, renew his strength, and heal what ails him in Your loving name.

Thank You, Lord.

Day 34

Hindrances

G od hears the prayers and requests of every person. After all, He is all knowing (omniscient). That, however, does not mean He accepts all requests on the same level. Indeed, there are hindrances in your life that can be displeasing to God and thus cause your prayers to be ineffective. To have an effective prayer life, you must make an effort to eliminate the hindrances to your prayers.

First and most importantly is to have a life reconciled with God through the death of His Son, Jesus Christ. Your relationship with God must be established with the acceptance that God sent His only Son to earth to live, die, and be resurrected for the forgiveness of our sins. The moment you come to Jesus for forgiveness and reconciliation, you are a beloved child of God. So, your goal is to have that right, joyful, and humble relationship with God by spending quality time with Him in thanksgiving for the gift of His Son.

The next obvious hindrance to effective prayers is sin. "If I had cherished sin in my heart, the Lord would not have listened" (Psalm 66.18). But the Lord will listen if you openly admit and confess your sins to Him and seek His forgiveness. "If we confess our sins, He is faithful and just and will forgive us our sins and purify us from all unrighteousness: (1 John 1.9). What an awesome God! Ask Him to forgive you with an honest request and done; He forgives you!

Another key hindrance to your prayers is unbelief. If you really don't expect God to answer your prayers, He probably won't. "O you of little faith" (Matthew 6.30). Why would you expect to receive anything from the Lord if deep down inside you don't think He can or will make it happen? Have faith, have trust in His Holy Word, BELIEVE He will respond to your requests. "If you believe, you will receive whatever you ask for in prayer" (Matthew 21.22).

Pride, self-esteem, and self -praise effectually shut the door of prayer. Approach God with humility and meekness.[99] Negligence, impatience, and fear will be fatal to your prayers.[100] There are many other hindrances to your prayer life, some of which are listed below for your consideration:

Selfish prayers.
Not asking according to God's will.
Losing heart or giving up.
Unforgiveness of others.
Frivolous prayers.
Hoping rather than having faith.
Doubt that your sins will be forgiven.
Doubt that your prayers will be answered.
Idols (anything you give higher priority than God).
Pride.
As you pray, ask yourself,
Is this the will of God?
Do you need to forgive someone?
Is your request for you or the glory of God?
Does your prayer contradict the Word of God?
Do you have faith in your request?

Father I pray to You and seek Your loving and helping heart to guide me in my prayers. Take away the faults I have that hinder me from coming closer to You. Open the gate to true communication with You and open my heart to hear You.

Note to self

_____
_____
_____
_____
_____
_____
_____

Day 35

Styles - Types - Components

The more you know about various styles, types, and formats of prayer, the more effective you can be in your personal prayer. No one style of prayer will fit every person. In fact, ANY style or format of prayer will most likely be modified to some degree to fit the individual. Indeed, you may totally change or at least modify the style of prayer you are using by the time you finish this 90 day devotional. Your goal is to spend time with God, so be prepared; you will make changes as you evolve in your prayer life.

The next several days will offer many options, styles, and formats of prayer. Each is unique in its presentation and participation just as you are unique as a person. I hope you will give each style a try as it comes up. Although you may be surprised at how many options there are to pray (and be assured, this devotional is not all-inclusive), you may find that having "options" and "variety" enhances your time with God. Variety takes away boredom that seems to creep into your time with God. But know this, not every style will fit your personality or needs. That's okay, just be open to new or different ideas. It is not a mistake that we each have different ways of communicating with God. He will lead you to the ultimate style of prayer best fitted for you and that which accomplish His purposes. "There are different kinds of working, but the same God works all of them in all men" (1 Corinthians 12.6).

The list of things to be considered in prayer could go on forever. There are, however, components that are critical for effective prayer. Each of the following will be discussed in more detail in the days to come:

Silence to begin your prayer time
Praise & Thanksgiving
Forgiveness of others
Confession of sin
Faith/Trust
Adoration
Listening
Love

Self examination: How are you doing? Write down your thought, wishes, and plans to improve.

_____
_____
_____
_____
_____
_____
_____
_____
_____
_____
_____
_____
_____
_____

Day 36

A.C.T.S.

A.C.T.S. is an acronym for Adoration, Confession, Thanksgiving, Supplications. This format of prayer is very popular around the world. It offers the basic components for a healthy prayer life.

ADORATION: Sets the tone for the entire prayer. It reminds you of who you are addressing, whose presence you have entered, and whose attention you have gained. It is the desire of your heart to worship, magnify, and bless God; you focus on nothing but His goodness. It gives you an opportunity to express how precious God is to you. Adoration reminds you of God's identity. It purges your spirit and prepares you to listen to God. In the adoration phase of this format, you ask for nothing, but seek only to profess God's goodness. Examples: God, You are all-knowing, all-caring, omnipotent, tender, forgiving, loving, the Creator, Savior, awesome, perfect, eternal, wise, gracious, faithful, patient, understanding, the King of all the earth. . . and the list goes on. You can also pick out a verse of Scripture to praise Him (Magnificat – Luke 1.46-55) (Zechariah's Song – Luke 1.68-79).

CONFESSION: Many people ask God to "forgive my many sins." You simply throw all your sins and faults into a single pile without so much as looking at them and ask God to "cover the whole dirty heap." This approach to confession is a cop out. When you lump all your sins together and confess them without name, it's not too painful or embarrassing. But if you take those sins out of the pile one by one and call them by name, well. . . . [101] Say it like it is. Name each sin, one by one, name by name. Your conscience will be cleansed, and you will be flooded with relief that God has a forgiving nature.

THANKSGIVING: Give thanks abundantly. Since you have just confessed your sins, He has given you something to be thankful for. Express your gratitude, give thanks to God for your many blessings: spiritual blessing, relational blessings, material blessings, and answered prayers.[102] Respond with joy to the benefits showered on you as His heir.

SUPPLICATIONS: You learned on day 28 that supplication means asking God for help, and is usually broken down into two parts: petitions (requests for yourself) and intercessions (asking requests for others). This is the time to tell God what you need and what you request of Him for others. An easy way to break down your requests is by category: ministry, people, family, and personal.[103]

Ministry: Church staff, ministries, executive boards.

People: Christian brothers & sisters, the sick, those far from God, etc.

Family: Spouses, children, parents, marriage, finances, education.

Personal: Your character (make me more like Christ).

The A.C.T.S. model is not perfect. To me there are other things to add, but they don't fit the acronym. In a few days you will have an opportunity to look at other "acronym" options. For now, enjoy this popular style of prayer!

A.C.T.S.

Besides being the acronym for a style of prayer, ACTS could also mean the Acts of the Apostles, the way I ACT, the way You want me to ACT. My desire is to ACT more like Jesus every day!

Day 37

Confession

As humans and ancestors of Adam, we all have sin. It is in our DNA. We certainly can and should do our best to eliminate sin, but the fact is it remains a part of us. "There is no one who does good, not even one" (Psalm 14.3). "There is no one righteous, not even one" (Romans 3.10). "There is not a righteous man on earth who does what is right and never sins" (Ecclesiastes 7.20). But through God's amazing love and the grace of Jesus Christ's blood, we can rest assured of our forgiveness and eternal rest in heaven.

If you confess your sins to God with true repentance and belief in the saving blood of Christ, your sins will be forgiven AND forgotten. "If we confess our sins, He is faithful and just and will forgive us our sins and purify us from all unrighteousness" (1John 1.9). "For I will forgive their wickedness and will remember their sins no more" (Hebrews 8.12).

Your confession of sin must come from your heart and be sincere. It comes from the inside out and must be honest. This is no time to pretend with God. He knows your every thought and action. "Nothing in all creation is hidden from God" (Hebrews 4.13). "For a man's ways are in full view of the Lord" (Proverbs 5.21). Surely you can see the foolishness of trying to hide or lessen your sins from God. Confess your wrongdoings openly and honestly, for God knows all about them before you ever say a word. It is in your confession that you are affirming to God that you recognize

Him as creator of everything, including His Son Jesus who gave His life for the redemption of sin.

Once you have honestly confessed your sin to God, feel assured and comforted that He has forgiven the sin and will remember it no more (Hebrews 8.12). Isn't that a wonderful feeling of assurance? If you have asked God to forgive you, He has forgiven you! If you are still carrying the sin around in your heart and mind, then you are doubting that God forgave you. That is why guilt comes back to life. The devil uses that guilt to undermine your faith.[104] It doesn't matter how terrible your offenses or how often you have failed – God blots out every sin when you sincerely ask for mercy.[105]

Remember this. . . . .

God chooses not to remember your sins once they have been forgiven. Don't bring up old baggage that God has already forgiven. Can't you just hear God saying, "What's this. . . I forgave that sin a long time ago. Why are you bringing it up again?"

At the Foot of the Cross by Don Moen

Psalm 51

This Psalm is a prayer of confession and repentance written by King David after his sin with Bathsheba (2 Samuel 11). This prayer serves as a good model for your confessional prayers.

We confess, then He forgives!

Day __38__

Confession 2 (faults)

Y ou can probably figure out the sins of life represented in the ten commandments (Deuteronomy 5), but what about the other "stuff" going on in your life? Anything that in any way separates you from God is sin, so consider your own personal, individual faults.

The seven deadly sins recognized throughout church history are not listed as such in the Bible:

Pride, Envy, Gluttony, Lust, Anger, Greed, Sloth.

There are also other possibilities of faults in your life. Do any of these fit you?

Self-centeredness, Judgmental, Hypocrisy, Controlling, Doubt, Arrogance, Jealousy, Failure to love others, Deception, Gossip, Boasting, Selfishness, Bitterness, Rage, Resentment, Slander, Stubbornness, Failure to forgive others, Lack of compassion for others, Vanity.

"There are six things the Lord hates, seven that are detestable to Him: haughty eyes, a lying tongue, hands that shed innocent blood, a heart that devises wicked schemes, feet that are quick to rush into evil, a false witness who pours out lies, and a man who stirs up dissension among brothers" (Proverbs 6.16).

> "Create in me a clean heart, O God,
> and renew a right spirit within me" (Psalm 51.10).

As you pray, ask God to build up and strengthen your:

Character – what you do when you think no one is watching.

Discipline – ask for inner strength to do what God's Word says.

Humility – remind you that "it's not about me."

Service – ask for a humble, helping heart.

Awareness – that God is in every detail of your life.

 Grace Flows Down by Christy Nockels

Most merciful God, I confess that I have sinned against you in thought, word, and deed, by what I have done, and by what I have left undone. I have not loved you with my whole heart; I have not loved my neighbor as myself. I am truly sorry and I humbly repent. For the sake of your Son Jesus Christ, have mercy on me and forgive me; that I may delight in your will, and walk in your ways, to the glory of your Name. Amen.[106]

Note to self

_____
_____
_____
_____
_____
_____
_____
_____
_____
_____
_____

Day 39

Forgiveness

Thank you, God, for forgiving me of my sins and faults. I certainly want forgiveness, but am I willing to forgive those who have offended me? Of course you know the next statement, the truth from the Bible, "For if you forgive men when they sin against you, your heavenly Father will also forgive you. But if you do not forgive men their sins, your Father will not forgive your sins" (Matthew 6.14-15). Think about it. This is a humbling thought. "Bear with each other and forgive whatever grievances you may have against one another. Forgive as the Lord forgave you" (Colossians 3.13).

"Father, forgive them, for they do not know what they are doing" (Luke 23.34). Jesus understood forgiveness. As He hung from the cross, after being beaten, whipped, scourged, and minutes away from His own death, He offers forgiveness to those persecuting Him. Could you do that? Don't come into God's presence and expect to have your prayers answered if you are asking God to forgive you of your sins, but you are refusing to forgive others.[107]

Forgiving another person first and foremost comes from within yourself. You must change yourself, your thoughts, your heart, releasing all anger and bitterness of the person and situation. In doing so, a freedom enters your heart and mind—finally giving you peace.

Forgiveness does not come easily for most of us. You naturally revert to self-protection and justification when you have been wronged or hurt. But forgiveness is a choice you have. If you choose to remain trapped in bitterness and hate, you are choosing to separate yourself from God. For God is love, and love has no hate. Forgiveness doesn't mean you will forget; however, you don't continue to use the memory against others. The offense will no longer control your behavior.[108] Forgiving someone does not mean you are releasing him or her from God's just judgment and punishment. But that is God's business, not yours. Yours is to forgive![109]

Forgiveness is your response to God, not to your fellow man. Your transgressor may not deserve it, desire it, or require it; yet you forgive because you know that your Father wants you to. Refusing to forgive is nothing less than disobedience to the Lord, and a sin against Him.[110]

Alas, know this; there is no lasting joy in forgiveness if it doesn't also include forgiving yourself. It is anything but total forgiveness if you forgive those who hurt you, but are unable to forgive yourself. It is as wrong as not forgiving others, because God loves you just as much as He loves others. He will be just as unhappy when you don't forgive yourself as when you hold a grudge against others.[111]

T.G.I.F.

Thank God I'm Forgiven
(Lord, help me forgive myself
and forgive others as You have forgiven me.)

Note to self

_____
_____
_____
_____
_____
_____
_____
_____
_____
_____
_____
_____

Day 40

Body Positions

Reverence and humility are always essential in your prayer time, so the heart is the central part of praying. But, the attitude of the body counts also.

The common practice of bowing your head and clasping your hands (or pressing your hands together with fingers pointing up) is a visible sign of your respect to God. Many people open their arms and turn their palms upward to receive God's outpouring of grace and love. Raising one or both hands high in the air is a sign of praise.

Kneeling is an indication of your submission to God. This is a favorite prayer position for many people. For those of us that are older, however, kneeling becomes painful to the back and knees if done for long periods of time. A prie dieu is a piece of furniture intended to enhance, and make more comfortable, the body position of kneeling while praying. A prie dieu (French: pronounced "pray do") is a type of prayer desk intended for private devotional use and is sometimes called a kneeler. A "prie dieu" is often used in the Catholic and Anglican churches.

Prostrate or lying flat on the floor (prone), either face up or face down, signifies submission and reverence.

Cross-legged, also known as the Buda or lotus position, is often used in meditative prayer. Sit cross-legged with your hands resting on your lap or resting on your knees with palms up.

Walking the labyrinth is one of the oldest contemplative forms of walking prayer. You walk slowly on a one-way pre-set course eventually coming to the end (usually in the center of the labyrinth).

Focus on setting one foot in front of the other, and on honoring God's presence with you on this journey. Ask His guidance in the prayer you use and seek His desire for you. For more information, Google: "labyrinth prayer."

Sitting in a chair, couch, or even recliner is certainly acceptable. Your body position during prayer need not be something you struggle with to meet some expectation you perceive others may have. Pray in a comfortable position. You may approach God with hearts that adore and glorify Him, whatever your body position is.[112]

What body position was used by individuals by some of the people in the Bible?

Daniel kneeled three times a day in prayer.
Solomon kneeled in prayer at the dedication of the temple.
Jesus prostrated Himself in the Garden of Gethsemane.

Some other examples listed in the Bible:

Sitting: 1 Chronicles 17.16-27
Kneeling: 1 Kings 8.54, Ezra 9.5, Luke 22.41, Acts 9.40
Bowing: Exodus 34.8, Nehemiah 8.6, Psalm 72.11
Standing: Nehemiah 9.5, Mark 11.25, Luke 18.13
Uplifted hands: 2 Chronicles 6.12-13, Psalm 63.4, 1 Timothy 2.8
Walking: 2 Kings 4.35
Prostrate: Joshua 7.6, Ezra 10.11, Matthew 26.39, Mark 14.35

The body positions you use in prayer should ultimately reflect the feelings of your heart!

Day 41

Create Your Own Style

There is no right way or wrong way to pray. The important thing is that you do pray. If the A.C.T.S. acronym or order of prayer does not fit your style, try creating your own. You can make your prayer style as personal as you like.

I, too, experiment from time to time with various "formats" of prayer. Variety is good; it keeps your prayer fresh. As you will also discover, I sometimes struggle with some formats of prayer; I just don't seem to "connect with God." You too may find that some formats just don't do it for you. That is okay. Experiment, listen to your heart, listen to God and focus on the style that brings you closest to Christ. Ask Him to lead you in the way He wants to talk to you.

Some other popular acronyms for prayer are:

B Blessings (to self & others)
A Adoration (acclaim God's goodness)
P Praise (glorify God)
T Thanksgivings (gratitude)
I Intercession (others and yourself)
S Sorry (ask for forgiveness of your sins)
M Meditation (listen to God)

P Praise
R Repent
A Ask
Y Yield

Bearpaw's favorites are: **H.U.N.T.E.R.** and **G.U.I.T.A.R.**

Prayer Acronym Helpers

A	Apply, adorn, atone, acclaim, adoration, ask
B	Boost, build-up, beatify, blessings
C	Confess, church, celebrations
D	Disappointments (sin & faults), disasters, devotion (praise)
E	Expose, exalt, enforce, edify, engage, exhibit, educate, emulate
F	Family, favors, finances, forgiveness
G	Gospel, glorify, God's presence
H	Honor, humble (humility), healing
I	Invite (God to join you), intercessions, improve (me)
J	Join (God join me), job (s)
K	Kudos (praise), kindness
L	Love, laws (broken)
M	Meditate, meditation
N	Needs, naughtiness, neglect
O	Oblations (thanksgivings), offerings, others (pray for)
P	Penitence, priest/pastor, petitions, praise, purpose
Q	Quest (to be like Jesus)
R	Read, repent, reveal, restore, regrets
S	Sacrifice, supplications, sick, sorry (sins), Spirit (Ps 51.10)
T	Thanksgivings
U	Ugliness, unfit, unload (sin)
V	Vows (promises)
W	Will (Your will be done), work (in need of)
X	X-tracate (my sins)
Y	Yield (may I yield to follow You)
Z	Zeal (to follow Your model)

Note to self

_____
_____
_____
_____
_____
_____
_____
_____
_____
_____

Day 42

You're Not Alone

Prayer defined in the Bible is:

A lifting up your soul to God (Psalm 25.1, 143.8)
A pouring out your heart to God (Psalm 62.8)
A crying out to God (Psalm 86.3)
Spiritual incense to God (Revelation 5.8)
Coming before the throne of grace (Psalm 84.1-2, Hebrews 4.16)
A spiritual sacrifice & the fruit of your lips (Hebrews 13.15)
Drawing close to God in friendship, fellowship, and trust (James 4.8)

There are hundreds of prayers in the Bible. In fact one source has totaled about 650 different prayers cited in Scripture.[113] There are also many passages in the Bible that have been sub-titled as "prayer of a specific person." It is these prayers that I am listing for your consideration of reading.

Blessed Lord, who caused all holy Scripture to be written for our learning: Grant us so to hear them, read, mark, learn, and inwardly digest them, that we may embrace and ever hold fast the blessed hope of everlasting life, which you have given us in our Savior Jesus Christ; who lives and reigns with you and the Holy Spirit, one God, for ever and ever. Amen.[114]

Please read the following prayers at your convenience:

€	1 Samuel 2.1-10	Hannah's Prayer
€	2 Samuel 7.18-29	David's Prayer
€	1 Kings 8.22	Solomon's Prayer
€	2 Kings 19.14	Hezekiah"s Prayer
€	1 Chronicles 4.10	Prayer of Jabez
€	1 Chronicles 17.16	David's Prayer
€	1 Chronicles 29.10	David's Prayer #2
€	Ezra 9.1	Ezra's Prayer
€	Nehemiah 1.4	Nehemiah's Prayer
€	Psalm 40.8	David's Prayer
€	Psalm 90	Prayer of Moses
€	Isaiah 37.14	Hezekiah's Prayer
€	Jeremiah 10.23	Jeremiah's Prayer
€	Daniel 9.3	Daniel's Prayer
€	Jonah 2.1	Jonah's Prayer
€	Habakkuk 3.1	Habakkuk's Prayer
€	John 17	Prayers of Jesus

 What A Friend We Have In Jesus

Note to self

_____
_____
_____
_____
_____
_____
_____
_____
_____
_____
_____

Day 43

Pharisee?

J esus said, "Be on your guard against the yeast of the Pharisees, which is hypocrisy" (Luke 12.1).

In the days of Jesus, the Pharisees were a political and religious sect numbering some 6,000 people. They were primarily blue collar, mostly poor, common Jewish people. The Pharisees most likely intended to obey God, but were very devoted and extreme in obedience of the Mosaic Law (the Torah: the first five books of the Bible) and Jewish tradition. They interpreted and adapted the written law of Moses to meet the conditions of the day and their own standards; thus creating what became known as the oral law.

The Pharisees opposed Jesus because He refused to accept their interpretations of the oral law. Jesus criticized the Pharisees on the grounds that, for all their commendable observance of rules and tradition, they were fundamentally unrepentant, neither knowing God nor loving people (Matthew 23).

The seven woes recited by Jesus refer to the Pharisees as hypocrites, pretending to be something they were not and performing their ministries only to be seen by other men (Matthew 23). The parable of the proud Pharisee:

Jesus said, "Two men went up to the temple to pray, one a Pharisee and the other a tax collector. The Pharisee stood up and prayed about himself: 'God, I thank you that I am not like other men – robbers, evildoers, adulterers, - or even like this tax collector. I fast twice a week and give a tenth of all I get.' But the tax collector stood at a distance. He would not even look up to heaven, but beat his breast and said, 'God, have mercy on me, a sinner.' I tell you that this man, rather than the other, went home justified before God. For everyone who exalts himself will be humbled, and he who humbles himself will be exalted" (Luke 18.9-14).

Today would be a good time for self- examination. What are YOUR motives? Ask yourself and think about:

Are you honest and sincere with God?
Why are you seeking a life of prayer?
To get material things you want?
To understand and love God—to become more like Jesus?
To be seen by others as reverent?
Do I tell others how much I pray so that I can lower them as I elevate myself?
Are you putting "time" in prayer so you can tell others how devout and pious you are?
Are you pretending to be something you are not?

Who are you when no one is looking? Though you may find it possible to deceive people in your life, God is never fooled.[115]
Are you a Pharisee?

> Lord Jesus, forgive me
> for acting like a Pharisee. . . . .

Note to self

_____
_____
_____
_____
_____
_____
_____
_____
_____
_____
_____
_____

Day 44

Scripture

Your belief is evidence that you trust God. He is not impressed by how many Scriptures you quote or how long you pray. He is moved and convinced when you believe what He has told you, and when you prove it by acting on it. Belief is trust in action.[116]

To use Scripture in your prayers means one thing; that you are familiar with Scripture. This means you must not only read the Bible, but also study it. Grrrrrr, not only are you asked to set aside time each day to pray, but you are also being asked to set aside time to read and study the Bible. So, "cowboy up and get 'r dun."

Whatever passage of Scripture you choose to meditate on, read it slowly, thoughtfully, and several times. As you begin, be sure to ask the Holy Spirit to enlighten your thoughts with His insights.[117] Using Scripture in your prayers is assurance that you are praying pleasing words to God and praying His will. You are honoring God through His own words and at the same time offering the gift of prayer for others.

You might consider memorizing passages of Scripture then using them as they apply in your prayers. Using God's word in prayer is about as close as you can get to speaking the language of Jesus Christ. As you weave His Word into your prayers you will bring His will and purpose to the forefront of your requests. Power in prayer is not based on emotions, feelings, or theories of man, but upon the Word of God.[118] Scripture says it so well, "Apply your heart to what I teach" (Proverbs 22.17).

The following list of special prayers and thanksgivings are from the New Testament for you to begin a study of Scripture.[119]

By whom	Reference	Subject
Apostles	Luke 17.5	For more faith
Apostles	Acts 1.24-25	On choosing an apostle
Blind Bartimaeus	Mark 10.47	For sight
Early church	Acts 4.24-30	Support under persecution
Father of boy	Matthew 17.15	For his only son
Jairus	Matthew 9.18	For his daughter
Jesus	Mt 11.25, Lk 10.21	Thanksgiving
Jesus	Mt 26.39 Lk 22.42	Suffering / Garden of Gethsemane
Jesus	Matthew 27.46	While feeling forsaken
Jesus	Luke 23.34	For His murderers
Jesus	Luke 23.46	Giving up His spirit to God
Jesus	John 11.41-42	Thanking His Father
Jesus	John 12.27-28	Asking for His Father's help
Jesus	John 17	For His apostles & believers
Lord's Prayer	Mt 6.9, Lk 11.2	A model for prayer
Paul	Acts 9.6-11	For instruction and grace
Paul	2 Cor 12.8	Relief from personal trial
Paul	Eph 1.17-20; 3.14-21; Phil 1.9-11; Col 1.9-11; 2 Thess 1.11-12; 2.16-17; 3.5; Heb 13.20-21	Intercession for churches
Criminal	Luke 23.42	To be remembered by Jesus
Pharisee's Prayer	Luke 18.11	Thanksgiving for righteousness
Prodigal son	Luke 15.18-19	For forgiveness
Tax collector	Luke 18.13	For divine mercy
Samaritan woman	John 4.15	For Living Water
Stephen	Acts 7.59-60	Forgiveness of murderers
Syrophoenician	Matthew 15.22	For her daughter
Ten lepers	Luke 17.13	For healing
The centurion	Matthew 8.6	For his servant
The disciples	Matthew 8.25	To be saved from the storm
The leper	Matthew 8.2	For healing
The royal official	John 4.40	For his child
The waiting church	Revelation 22.20	For the coming of Christ
Two blind men	Matthew 9.27	For sight

Day __45__

Excuse Me!

"No, seriously, I don't have time to pray. You can't believe how hectic and stressful my life is. . .," says you.

If you have heard it once, you have heard it a hundred times, "Excuses are a dime a dozen." I know, I know:

You have a demanding job.
You have two jobs, or three.
Your kids take up all your spare time.
You are too tired.
The big game is on tonight.
You would have to get up earlier.

Maybe you are going to play your "I'm only a kid" card – or, "I don't know how to pray" (lucky you, read the rest of this book).

I have homework.
I have after school activities.
I don't go to church.
Real men don't pray (WHAT???)
Yada - yada - yada : (

Remember this: Your excuses are praised by Satan because he does not want you to have a relationship with God.

Prayer is something that takes time, effort, and discipline – and regardless of your situation, it can be done. It all comes down to what your priorities are. You see, we all make time for the things that are important to us. Our busyness seldom keeps us from eating or sleeping.[120] In prayer you basically do two things, ask and listen, yet you struggle to slow down long enough to spend time with God.[121] You convince yourself that you are just too busy (or yada – yada – yada) to pray. Spend a few moments today thinking about what your priorities really are. Of course family and career are important, but just where do you put God on your list?

If you don't feel like praying, make an effort to do so anyway. God knows your lack of motivation to pray, but you are showing your love of God and faith by showing up to pray anyway. When you get right down to it, the only reason for not praying is if you do not believe in God. Is that your excuse? Are you saying you don't really love God enough to spend time with Him each day?

E.G.O.

Edging **O**ut **G**od

Dear Jesus,

How desperately I need to learn to pray. And yet when I am honest, I know that I often do not even want to pray. I am distracted. I am stubborn. I am self-centered. I am proud. Bring me more in line with You so I can come to what I need.

Note to self

_____
_____
_____
_____
_____
_____
_____
_____
_____
_____
_____

Day 46

Popcorn Prayers

Y ou do not have to wait until your "scheduled" prayer time to offer prayer; pray as a need arises. When something just "pops up" and you feel the need, then it is time to pray! This may be an unexpected situation that has happened in your life, or your community, or the world – or it may be something you were already aware of and feel the need to pray "at that moment."

Popcorn prayers are spontaneous and "pop up" (popcorn; get it?) at any time throughout the day. They are certainly not intended to replace your individual, private, scheduled, uninterrupted time with God each day. Instead, they offer opportunities to meet the words of Scripture at other times of the day. Paul said in his letter to the Thessalonians, "Pray continually" (1 Thessalonians 5.17). He also said to the Christians of Corinth, "Devote yourself to prayer, being watchful and thankful" (Colossians 4.2). As the long-standing motto of the Boy Scouts of America says, "Be prepared." There are so many opportunities throughout the day to talk to God: driving by a cemetery, when you pass a car wreck or ambulance, at work when you answer the phone, worse yet - at home when you answer the phone at 2:00 am, when a disaster or tragedy occurs, when your friend calls and tells you they have cancer, when traveling in bumper-to-bumper traffic, for an amber alert, as you are cooking or doing the dishes, as you brush your teeth or watch your child sleep, for thanksgivings that happen during the day, and so on. Popcorn prayers are usually short, brief prayers – but they don't have to be. As with all prayer, there are NO rules. Pray as you feel called.

I live in the state of Colorado, and big game hunting is a part of my life (hence, the name Bearpaw). For decades I have always taken a pocket edition of the Bible to read in camp and in the field. You would be surprised how often reading Scripture leads to prayers of intercession and thanksgiving!

Another "format" of popcorn prayers is in a group or community setting. Usually the leader of the prayer session begins by saying a short sentence, to be followed by whoever is moved. There is no specific order (although you could reply in order as you go around the room or circle). An example might be something like this: Leader, "Father God, in my job help me to. . .," or "Lord, I ask your forgiveness for. . .," or "O God, thank you for. . . ." Then the people in the group reply as they feel called with one word or short sentences as a response to the statement as it relates to them.

Another group "format" of popcorn prayers is to just have the people in the group "pop up" at random, one at a time, with short prayers with no specific lead-in.

Popcorn prayer is the name I use for these types of quick, spontaneous prayers. They are sometimes referred to as "arrow prayers" or "flash prayers" also. The name is not important. Just know that you are not restricted to your "devoted prayer time" to offer concerns and thanks to our wonderful God. He is happy to hear from you at any time for any reason.

Note to self

_____
_____
_____
_____
_____
_____
_____
_____
_____

Day 47

5

There are a few prayer styles I would like to share with you that relate to "5". The number five in the Bible is significant because God's creation, man, has five fingers, five senses, and five toes. Thus it is the number of God's grace. There are five great mysteries: Father, Son, Spirit, Creation, and Redemption. After the fall of man, creation was cursed and it became subject to vanity. So man and creation needed to be redeemed; therefore, the number 5 is the number of God's grace and redemption. [122]

Five Finger Prayer[123]

In this style of prayer each finger on your hand serves as a reminder for a specific group of people for whom you should pray:

Thumb :   people closest to you.
Pointing finger :   teachers and leaders of ministries.
Tallest finger :   civic and government leaders
Ring finger :   the weak and downtrodden
Little finger :   your needs.

Of course, you could certainly modify the format to fit your own needs and the "titles" for each of the fingers. For example, the topics of prayer might be: family, those in need of healing, those in need of financial help or employment, those who have experienced disasters & tragedies, and thanksgivings.

5

Five Senses Prayer[124]

This technique uses your senses as a guide to focus your prayers on:

Hearing : hearing and discerning God's voice.
Touch : sharing the Good News of Jesus Christ with others around you.
Smell : becoming more sensitive to sin.
Sight : meeting the needs of others.
Taste : experiencing the fullness and joy of God.

Five Family Favorites

A form of prayer that involves the entire family at meal time or family devotional time is to have each person make 5 responses to the question of the day. The question might be, "What do you have to be thankful for today?" Or it could be, "What concerns do you have that you need help with?" Or, "Who would you like to pray for today?" The possibilities for questions are endless; just choose something that seems appropriate for your family that day.

> Do you remember the 5 powerful words from day 32?
>
> **Can I Pray For You?**

Note to self

_____
_____
_____
_____
_____

Day 48

Be Quiet!

Contemplative Prayer – Centering Prayer – Meditative Prayer

W hen most people think of contemplative, meditative, or centering prayer, they think of monks, nuns, monasteries, or being alone in a dark sanctuary with only a candle burning. This thought is certainly a part of those people's lives, but in reality it is a genuine consideration for all Christians in their prayer life. The idea of "being quiet" and giving "control" of your prayers and thoughts may sound a little scary at first. After all, you live in a world of hustle and bustle, constant communication, and. . . . noise. Deep reflection on a sacred thought, devotional, or Scripture is not something you may be comfortable with. However, as you spend more and more time in this form of prayer, you slowly become more drawn to the silence, solitude, and simplicity.

Contemplative prayer is the one discipline that can free you from your addiction to words. It immerses you into the silence of God.[125] This type of prayer involves no words, but rather submitting your heart and mind to God's direction and transformation.

Centering prayer is but one aspect of contemplative or meditative prayer. It could best be defined as the first step of contemplative prayer – preparing for the gift of contemplation. This gives you a way to respond to God without words and to allow the Holy Spirit to enter your heart and mind.

Thomas Ward outlines how to practice the discipline of centering prayer:[126]

1. Choose a sacred word as the symbol of your intention to consent to God's presence and action within.
2. Sitting comfortably and with your eyes closed, settle briefly and silently. Introduce the sacred word as the symbol of your consent to God's presence and action within.
3. When you become aware of thoughts, return ever-so-gently to the sacred word.
4. At the end of the prayer period, remain in silence with your eyes closed for several minutes.

It is suggested you spend at least 20 minutes in quiet meditation.

My Dear Father,

I am not used to being quiet.
Honestly, I'm not sure I can be quiet for 20 minutes.
As I submit my thoughts and control to You,
give me courage and strength.
I know You are with me, for You said,
"I will not leave you" (Genesis 28.15).

Shhhhhhh, be quiet!

Day 49

Lectio Divina

Lectio Divina (a Latin term meaning "divine reading") is a kind of reading in which the mind descends into the heart. It is a style of meditative / contemplative prayer in which you allow the Holy Spirit to lead your thoughts.

One procedure of Lectio Divina is to choose a passage of Scripture and read it slowly and in contemplation. Take a minute of silence focusing mentally on the passage and what word(s) stand out in your mind.

Read the passage again. This time, take two minutes of silence, allowing the Holy Spirit to impress upon you what you "hear", "see", "feel", and "sense."

Finally, read the passage slowly a third time. Take three minutes of silence and listen to God's direction concerning the passage.

Another method of Lectio Divina is the 4-part format: Read, Meditate, Pray, Contemplate.

Read: Again, read the chosen passage of Scripture slowly and perhaps several times. You are seeking the Holy Spirit's guidance in revealing the Word of God to you. You are letting go of your agenda and opening your heart and mind to what God wants to say to you.

Meditate: Yes, Lectio Divina requires reading, but your ultimate goal is primarily to listen to the Holy Spirit. This is not Bible study where you break down every word or sentence you read. Instead, allow God and the Holy Spirit to lead your thoughts. At first you will probably want to analyze the reading. Be patient and listen; wait for the Holy Spirit to illuminate your thoughts as you meditate on the passage.

Pray: Leave your thoughts behind and simply let your heart speak to God. After being led by the Holy Spirit, your prayer is inspired by the reflection on the Word of God

Contemplation: Now let go of everything in your being: your thoughts, your ideas, your plans – everything. Simply rest in the Word of God. You are now listening at the deepest level and gradually being transformed from within. This transformation will have a profound effect on the way you live.

Prayer starter:

Lord Jesus, allow me to slow down and listen to You. Take my hand and lead me, give me peace, give me relaxation. . . . .

Try me :)

If you don't have a passage of Scripture in mind, try this passage as you experiment with the Lectio Divina style of prayer: "Hear, O Israel: The Lord our God, the Lord is one. Love the Lord your God with all your heart and with all your soul and with all your strength. These commandments that I give you today are to be upon your hearts. Impress them on your children. Talk about them when you sit at home and when you walk along the road, when you lie down and when you get up. Tie them as symbols on your hands and bind them on your foreheads. Write them on the doorframes of your houses and on your gates" (Deuteronomy 6.4-9).

(This passage is known as the Shema (Hebrew for "hear"); it has become the Jewish confession of faith, still today recited by pious Jews).[127]

Day 50

Prayer Beads

One tool of prayer to help keep you focused is prayer beads. You hold them in your hand, progressing from bead to bead as you say your prayers. They help keep you organized, on task, and provide a sense of comfort and closeness to Christ. Major religions have for centuries advocated the use of prayer beads as an aid to prayer. Interestingly, the old English word "bede" means prayer. The Desert Fathers of the 3rd and 4th centuries used knotted ropes to count prayers, typically the Jesus Prayer (which will be introduced to you on Day 61).

There are different kinds of prayer beads, depending on your faith denomination – and some vary in design. You may be familiar with the Catholic prayer beads or rosary which has 59 beads. Orthodox rosaries have up to 100 beads. Anglican or "Christian Prayer Beads" have 33 beads. The use of prayer beads dates back to the Egyptians in around 3200 BC, while the Anglican / Protestant beads were not developed until mid-1980s. It is the Anglican Prayer Beads that I wish to focus on today. Below is a diagram of the Anglican Prayer Beads.

The Anglican Prayer Beads are more than simple recitation or prayers. In fact, the use of the beads is limited only to your imagination.

The Anglican Prayer Beads have a set of 33. This repr sents the number of years in Christ's life. The Anglican Prayer Beads consist of four sets of 7 beads called "weeks". The number 7 represents wholeness and completion and reminds us of the 7 days of creation, the 7 days of the temporal week, the 7 seasons of the church year (Advent, Christmas, Epiphany, Lent, Holy Week, Easter, and Pentecost), and the 7 sacraments (Holy baptism, Holy Eucharist, Confirmation, Ordination, Marriage, Unction, Penance). Four larger "cruciform" beads separate the "weeks". They represent the 4 points of the cross and its centrality in our lives and faith, the 4 seasons of the temporal year, and the 4 points on a compass. Near the cross is the "invitatory" bead.

Some Prayer Suggestions

The Cross: In the name of God, Father , Son, and Holy Spirit. Amen.

The Invitatory (1 bead): Let the words of my mouth and the meditation of my heart be acceptable in your sight, O Lord, my strength and my Redeemer. (Psalm 19.14)
    Memory: I come to You humbly seeking to be more like You.

The Cruciforms (4 large beads): O Lamb of God, that takest away the sins of the world, have mercy on me. O Lamb of God, that takest away the sins of the world, have mercy on me. O Lamb of God, that takest away the sins of the world, grant me your peace.
    Memory: Open my heart to receive Your Word and may it take action in my life.

The Weeks (7 smaller beads X 4 weeks): Father God, thank you for your love and your presence with me, today and always.
    Memory: recite verse and passage of Scripture.

Alternative method of praying the "weeks": Choose 4 topics (family, healing, disasters, God's presence, etc.) and 7 people in each week to pray for under that topic. If you choose more than four topics, you may make as many rotations around the beads as you would like to.
    Memory: Recite a passage of Scripture to memory (ie: Matthew 28.20 "I am always with you.") Each week of the year, change the Scripture for new memorization. (a great way to memorize Scripture).

Day 51

Psalms

Psalms has often been called the "Prayer Book" of the Bible. The Psalms contain every human emotion, even negative and hurtful ones. Praying the Psalms can confront you with things in yourself you had not known were there. Let the phrases of the Psalms filter slowly through your mind. What is God saying to you through the Psalm?[128]

There are 150 Psalms in the Bible. The traditional Hebrew title was *tehillim* (praises), although many of the Psalms are actually *tephillot* (prayers). The title "Psalms" was first used in the Septuagint (translation of the Hebrew Bible into Greek).[129] I encourage you to read each of the Psalms and take note of the numerous emotions of joy, sadness, praise, anger, song, thanksgiving, confession, and others. I suggest reading one book of Psalms each day.

God's Word was written to be studied, understood, and applied, and the Book of Psalms lends itself most directly to application. They put into words your deepest hurts, longings, thoughts, and prayers. They gently push you toward being what God designed you to be – people-loving and living for Him.[130]

Read one of the books of Psalms; then choose a verse(s) that stuck out in your mind. Using one of the contemplative / meditative prayer methods, allow God to speak to you about the passage. If you don't have a pre-selected verse of Psalms, try Psalm 51.

A few Psalms about prayer:

4.1	42.8	69.13	109.4
5.1	54.2	80.4	109.7
6.9	55.1	84.8	122.6
17.1	55.17	86.6	141.2
17.6	61.1	88.2	141.5
32.6	65.2	88.13	143.1
35.13	66.19	102.1	154.18
39.13	66.20	102.17	

The seven penitential Psalms:

6	38	102	148
32	51	130	

Popular Psalms:

3.3-4	27.1	55.22	116.14-15
4.3	27.4	59.17	188.5
5.3	29.2	63.3-4	118.7
5.11-12	31.5	68.4	119.105
8.3-5	32.8	71.9	130.5
9.1	34.1-2	73.23	139.23
13.16	37.3-5	73.26	139.24
16.7-8	37.16	91.11-12	145.8
16.11	39.4	100.2	145.14
18.3	40.3	100.3	147.4
19.14	46.1-2	100.4-5	147.11
23.1+	46.10	103.10	150.6
24.1	51.2	103.11-12	
25.4-5	51.10	116.8	

Note to self

Day 52

The Lord's Prayer
The Paternoster (Latin)

The Lord's Prayer is an excellent model for prayer, but it was never intended to be a magical incantation to get God's attention. He gave it as a pattern to suggest the variety of elements that should be included when you pray.[131] When Jesus said, "Pray in this way," He was giving the disciples a *way* to pray, not a prayer to pray. He was teaching the disciples an index (outline) of the various topics to be covered in prayer.[132] Many say this prayer should not even be called the Lord's Prayer since it does not apply to Him (for we know Jesus never had nor ever will have sin). Those who say this would offer that John 17 would be a more likely option for the Lord's Prayer. Regardless of its name, the prayer we call the Lord's Prayer offers much more than we often consider.

The Lord's Prayer is written in two of the Gospels: Matthew 6.9-13 and the shorter version in Luke 11.2-4. This prayer has been analyzed and dissected by hundreds of people. . . in fact, entire books have been written about it. Following is one simple breakdown of the Lord's Prayer.[133]

Sentence	Topic
Our Father in heaven, Hallowed be your name	worship
Your kingdom come	allegiance
Your will be done on earth as it is in heaven	submission

Give us today our daily bread	petition & provision
Forgive us our debts as we have forgiven our debtors	forgiveness
And lead us not into temptation, but deliver us from the evil one	watchfulness & deliverance
For Yours is the kingdom and the power and the glory, forever and ever. Amen (added later)	worship

Bill Hybels explains the Lord's Prayer like this:[134]

Our Father – never forget you are praying to your Father.

Who art in heaven – reminder that God is sovereign, majestic, and omnipotent (unlimited power or authority). Nothing is too big for Him.

Hallowed be Thy name – worship God and praise Him when you come to prayer. Don't let your prayers turn into a wish list.

Thy kingdom come, Thy will be done, on earth as it is in heaven – submit your will to God's. Put His will first in your life.

Give us this day our daily bread – lay out all your concerns, big and small.

Forgive us our trespasses, as we forgive those who trespass against us – be sure you are not the obstacle, confess your sins.

Lead us not into temptation, but deliver us from evil – pray for protection from evil and victory over temptation.

For Thine is the kingdom, and the power, and the glory forever – begin and end your prayer with more worship and praise. Remember, this is all about God; acknowledge that everything in heaven and earth is His.

Amen – let it be so.

The Lord's Prayer by Selah

Day __53__

Adoration

"Hallow God's Name"

To adore God is to praise Him, to honor Him for His greatness. To "bless the Lord" is a Biblical way of putting it. There is a difference between adoration and thanksgiving. One way to think of it is like this; we praise God for who He is, we thank God for what He has done for us. The emphasis in adoration is God's greatness.[135]

Prayer honors God, acknowledges His being, exalts His power, adores His providence, and secures His aid. In other words, it ADORNS Him.[136]

A simple yet classic prayer of adoration comes from St. Francis of Assisi. Francis was an Italian Catholic Friar and Priest. He founded the men's Franciscan Order and the women's Order of St. Clare. He lived from 1182-1226. Following is his prayer of adoration:

Lord God:
You alone are holy,
You who work wonders!
You are strong, you are great,
You are Most High,
You are the almighty King,
You, holy Father, King of heaven and earth.
Lord God, you are Three and you are One,

You are goodness, all goodness,
You are the highest good,
Lord God, living and true.
You are love and charity, you are wisdom,
You are humility, you are patience,
You are beauty, you are sweetness,
You are safety, you are rest, you are joy,
You are our hope,
And our delight,
You are justice, you are moderation,
You are all our wealth and riches overflowing.
You are beauty, you are gentleness,
You are our shelter, our guard
And our defender,
You are strength, you are refreshment,
You are our hope,
You are our faith,
You are our love,
You are our complete consolation,
You are our life everlasting,
Great and wonderful Lord,
All powerful God, merciful Savior.
Amen.

 How Great Is Our God
DVD by Louie Giglio

Note to self

Day 54

The Prayer of Jabez

Jabez cried out to the God of Israel, "Oh, that you would bless me and enlarge my territory! Let your hand be with me, and keep me from harm so that I will be free from pain" (1 Chronicles 4.10). "And God granted his request" (1 Chronicles 4.10).

Dr. Bruce Wilkinson authored a book entitled The Prayer Of Jabez that I encourage you to read. I will summarize his thoughts as best as I can.[137]

There are four requests in this prayer:

1. Bless me
2. Enlarge my territory
3. Be with me
4. Keep me from evil (harm)

BLESS ME: This may not be as self-centered as you think. To "bless" in the days of Jabez meant to fill with benefits, either as an end in itself or to make the object blessed a source of further blessing for others.[138] In a sense, you are asking for God's will as evidenced by Jabez's not asking for certain blessings of what, when, where, and how.

ENLARGE MY TERRITORY: This is not asking for more land, more gifts, or more responsibility / control. Rather you are asking God to enlarge your life so you may be a better vessel for God's use.

BE WITH ME: Here, you affirm God's great power (omnipotence) and ask that His will be done. In all that He does, you offer glory and praise to Him. You are asking God to provide power to work through your human weaknesses.

KEEP ME FROM EVIL: Ask God for protection from Satan's evil attacks that prevent you from doing God's will.

> "If you believe, you will believe
> whatever you ask for in prayer."
> (Matthew 21.22)

We will talk more about "faith" later, but Scripture tells you over and over that to receive an answer from God you must **believe** that He exists, is all powerful, and will do everything He says He will do – including answering your prayers. So, Dr. Wilkinson concludes his book about Jabez's prayer by suggesting a thirty day plan. He encourages you to follow this plan unwaveringly:[139]

1. Pray the Jabez Prayer every morning and keep a record of your daily prayer by marking a calendar or a chart you make especially for the purpose.
2. Write out the prayer and keep it in your Bible, in your day-timer, (added by Bearpaw—on your cell phone), on your bathroom mirror, or some other place where you will be reminded of your new vision.
3. Tell one other person of your commitment to your new prayer habit, and ask him or her to check up on you each week.
4. Begin to make a record of changes in your life, especially divine appointments and new opportunities you can relate directly to the Jabez Prayer.
5. Start praying the Jabez Prayer for your family, friends, and local church.

Day 55

Prayer of St. Francis

Francis Bernardone was born in 1182 in Assisi, Italy. In 1204 he had a vision and was called to live a life of poverty and prayer. He founded the Franciscan Order in 1210 and later the women's Order of St. Clare. Francis died in 1226 and was pronounced a saint by Pope Gregory IX in 1228. He is known as the Patron Saint of Animals, the Environment, and Italy. He is also known for his love of the Eucharist, his sorrow during the Stations of the Cross, for the creation of the Christmas Crèche or Nativity Scene, and his obvious belief in and love for prayer.

A famous prayer called "the Prayer of St. Francis" first appeared around 1915 and embodies the spirit of St. Francis of Assisi's simplicity and poverty. It most likely was not written by St. Francis. Some say it was attributed to St. Francis because it was found to be written on a Holy Card of St. Francis during World War II. The prayer bore no name or author, and became known as the Prayer of St. Francis because of this Holy Card. Regardless of who the author is, it is a beautiful prayer.

Prayer of St. Francis
Lord, make me an instrument of thy peace;
Where there is hatred, let me sow love;
Where there is injury, pardon;
Where there is doubt, faith;
Where there is despair, hope;
Where there is darkness, light;

And where there is sadness, joy.

As a man of prayer, St. Francis authored many prayers, of which only a few are listed here:

<u>Prayer of Self Giving</u>
I beg you, Lord, let the fiery,
gentle power of your love
Take possession of my soul,
And snatch it away from
everything under heaven,
That I may die for your love
As you saw fit to die for mine.

<u>Prayer Before a Crucifix</u>
(Almost all manuscripts that contain this simple prayer
indicate its origin at the foot of the crucifix in the Church of
San Damiano).
Most high, glorious God
Enlighten the darkness of my heart and give me, Lord,
A correct faith, a certain hope, a perfect charity,
sense and knowledge,
so that I may carry out Your holy and true command. Amen.

 Make Me A Channel Of Your Peace
(Prayer of St. Francis)

As you listen to this song, think about and meditate on the words of this prayer.

Day 56

Praise / Thanksgiving

Ever felt like you have nothing to pray for? Remember the verse 1 Thessalonians 5.17 (with thanksgiving) or Philippians 4.6 (but in everything, by prayer and petition, with thanksgiving, present your requests to God)? Pray with thanksgiving!! Giving thanks is the very life of prayer. Thankful prayers provide a solid foundation on which you can build all other prayers. Plus, a grateful attitude makes it easier for you to communicate with God.[140]

Praise is expressing to God your appreciation and understanding of His worth. It is saying "thank you" for each aspect of His divine nature. Your inward attitude becomes outward expressions. When you praise God, you help yourself by expanding your awareness of who He is.[141] King David said, "I will praise you, O Lord, with all my heart" (Psalm 9.1).

When you thank God for the many pleasures He provides, you are affirming that He is the Almighty from whom all blessings flow. It is impossible to praise or thank God too much![142] While prayer looks to the future, thanksgiving deals with things already received. Prayer deals with things desired, asked for, and expected. Prayer turns to gratitude and praise when the things asked for have been granted by God.[143]

Regardless of what is going on in your life at the present time, take the time to thank God and praise Him for what He has done in your life and will continue to do. When you are lying awake at night worrying about what you can't change, pour out your heart to God, and thank Him that He is in control.[144]

Go back to Day 25 and read again the part about spending ETERNITY in heaven with people you may not enjoy while here on earth. You may very well be worshiping God with those you will love dearly when you are in heaven with them. Praise and thanksgiving will be your blessed employment while you remain in heaven, and you will **never** grow weary of this pleasing task.[145]

Chris Tiegreen[146] notes a good point in the first line of the Lord's Prayer (Matthew 6.9). Although most describe this opening statement as an act of adoration, Tiegreen suggests it is also a glorious introduction of praise and says that your prayers should begin with praise! If you want your prayers to align with God's will, you must acknowledge truth at every turn. And the first step in acknowledging truth is declaring His primacy and His worth. You pray to your intimate Father because He is hallowed and holy, the Name above all names. You might as well set that straight in your own heart before you bombard Him with petitions, intercessions, and requests.

Louis Cassels says adoration (praise) is the highest form of prayer. Is praise the cornerstone, the centerpiece of your prayers? The rest of your prayers should revolve around your giving glory, thanks, and praise to God. If you need to realign your prayer "style", now is the time to do that. . . . thank God for all He has done for you!

Try this. . . . .

Each of the 34 days left in this devotional cycle make a point to offer at least *one prayer of thanksgiving* each day for the innumerable blessings God has bestowed upon you. I think you will be amazed at how your attitude and life will change – and hopefully "thanksgiving" will become a part of your daily life.

Day 57

Sing Praises!

"He who sings, prays twice"
(St. Augustine)

Most, if not all Christians, are addicted to music; of course not all the same genre. We know music has the power to influence our feelings and emotions. You may say, "I'm not a good singer." God doesn't care what you sound like (P. S. – He'll fix that when you get to heaven!) He is more interested in what your heart sounds like.

Singing/music is yet another form of worshiping our God. The main purpose of singing is for God's ear. Certainly it is not for the glorification of the choir or "band", nor to draw people to church, but it is for the glory of God and the good of the souls in the congregation.[147] The conscience presence of God inspires song, and so spiritual singing is not done by musical talent or taste, but rather by the grace of God in the heart of the singer. All music is to the Lord, for His glory, and in His honor.[148]

Not only does music glorify God, it often touches the inner most being of you! From the old classic hymns of yester-year, to the modern praise music of today, the words and music of praying through song settle deep within your heart, many times bringing tears of joy to your eyes as you meditate on the words. It is at this time that you are "praying twice to God" through your voice and through your heart.

I personally learned to play the guitar at the age of 55. I had NO background in music prior to that. As the old saying goes, "I couldn't even play the radio well." Six years later I often play at the worship service at our church and play almost daily at home in the honor and glory of God. As a member of the church Praise Team, I have taken the time to read and research where many of the hymns and songs derived from. I often read that Scripture before and after playing and singing it several times. Maybe he who sings, prays THRICE (from the heart, vocally, and by reading Scripture)!

 As We Worship You by Don Moen

Consider. . . . .

Music can help you recall words and ideas you might otherwise forget. Consider what God might want you to remember about Him. Is it His power, His holiness, His love, or His faithfulness? Can you think of a song that celebrates God's character?[149]

"Sing and make music in your heart to the Lord" (Ephesians 5.19).

Day __58__

Sing Praises! 2

L et us worship the Lord in song. There are over 500 passages of Scripture that relate to song or music. Following are some passages that may be of interest:

Scripture	Main Text
Exodus 15.1	Moses and the people of Israel sang this song to the Lord, "I will sing to the Lord, for He is highly exalted."
Psalm 13.6	I will sing to the Lord, for He has been good to me.
Psalm 33.3	Sing to Him a new song, play skillfully, and shout for joy.
Psalm 47.6	Sing praises to God, sing praises; sing praises to our King, sing praises.
Psalm 68.4	Sing praises, sing praises to His name.
Psalm 95.1-2	Come, let us sing for joy to the Lord; let us shout aloud to the Rock of our salvation. Let us come before Him with thanksgiving and extol Him with music and song.
Psalm 100.2	Worship the Lord with gladness; come before Him with joyful songs.
Psalm 104.33	I will sing to the Lord all my life; I will sing praise to my God as long as I live.
Psalm 144.9	I will sing a new song to you, O God.
Psalm 147.1	How good it is to sing praises to our God!
Psalm 150.1-6	Praise God with trumpet, harp, lyre, tambourine, dancing, strings, flute, and cymbals.

Isaiah 12.5	Sing to the Lord, for He has done glorious things.
Zeph 3.17	He will rejoice over you with singing.
Matthew 26.30	When they had sung a hymn, they went out to the Mount of Olives.
Acts 16.25	About midnight Paul and Silas were praying and singing hymns to God.
Romans 15.9	I will sing hymns to your name.
1 Cor 14.15	I will sing with my spirit, I will sing with my mind.
Ephesians 5.19	Sing and make music in your heart to the Lord.
Colossians 3.16	Sing psalms, hymns, and spiritual songs with gratitude in your hearts to God.
James 5.13	Is anyone happy? Let him sing songs of praise.

Below are PSALMS that relate to music or singing:

7.17	45.8	96.1	135.3
9.2	47.6	96.2	138.1
9.11	66.2	98.1	144.9
13.6	66.4	98.5	146.2
18.49	68.4	98.9	147.1
28.7	68.32	101.1	147.7
30.4	69.30	105.2	149.1
32.11	81.1	108.1	149.3
33.1	89.1	108.3	149.5
40.3	95.1	118.14	150.4
42.8	95.2	119.172	

 I Will Sing by Don Moen

133

Day 59

Book of Common Prayer

The Book of Common Prayer is a book of some 1,000 pages originally introduced in 1549 containing a collection of both old and new prayers. It is used by the Episcopal Church in the United States, the Anglican Church in England, and worldwide by many Christians of various faith denominations. It contains the "Daily Office," Scripture readings, canticles, seasonal prayers. It is read every day in many seminaries, monasteries, parish churches, and by individuals at home.[150]

Definitions that may be helpful as you learn about the Book of Common Prayer:

Canticle – a hymn whose words are taken from the Bible, used in certain church services.

Collect – a short prayer often used in church services especially before the reading of Scripture.

Compline – the last of the seven canonical hours assigned to prayer (matins, prime, terce, sext, none, vespers, and compline).

Daily Devotions – shorter versions of morning or evening prayer.

Daily Office – a prayer service for morning and/or evening (often called Morning Prayer or Evening Prayer).

Office – means service (as in a worship service or prayer service).

Prayers of the People – Six different scripted and formatted prayer offerings.

Propers – prayers for a particular day or church season.

Psalter – Book of Psalms.

The Book of Common Prayer also includes a service for Noonday Prayers, an order for worship in the evening (short version), an order for compline (end of the day), daily devotions for individuals or families, collects, propers, forms of confession, worship services, liturgies for special days (Ash Wednesday, Palm Sunday, Maundy Thursday, Good Friday, Holy Saturday, The Great Easter Vigil), the Psalter, prayers and thanksgivings, and more. This book is truly a multi-faceted book of value to almost any faith denomination. The Book of Common Prayer may be purchased at almost any book-store, at Amazon.com, or on-line at www.anglican.org.

If you are interested in trying one of the Daily Offices (Morning Prayer and/or Evening Prayer) to see if you like the format, or as an "every day" practice, you may go on-line to:

justice.anglican.org

D.O.G.
Depend **O**n **G**od

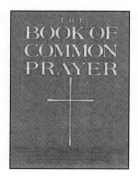

Day 60

Day 60

Wow, day 60! Let's take a survey of your progress.

€   Are you still standing firm to your Day 1 commitment to give God part of your life every day? If you have been faithful, congratulations! You are nearing your desire to create the habit or routine to be with God every day and making that commitment a true passion! If you have failed, God understands. Start up again where you left off.

€   Sing a song of praise to your Lord. Listen to a Christian radio station and sing along.

€   Are you a Pharisee? Are you pretending to be someone you are not?

€   "Can I Pray For You?" Have you offered to pray for someone?

€   Are you "talking" to God and giving honor and glory to Him through praise and thanksgiving?

€   Have you tried using prayer beads for Scripture memorization? You can purchase prayer beads or buy some beads and a cross and make your own. Refer back to Day 50 for more information.

As you have discovered, changing your routine to include daily prayer and time with God requires discipline and effort. It is not always easy, and if you are like me, excuses for not praying linger on your thoughts often. Be strong and courageous (Deuteronomy 31.6). There are only 30 days left in this devotional. It is important to realize that changing a habit or routine in your daily life is much more than simply reading information. That alone is not powerful enough to create a routine. A true change in behavior obviously starts with God opening your heart to a new routine and your willingness and desire to make that change happen. Is this transformation happening in your life? Are you allowing God to speak to you in His effort to bring you closer to Him? Sit quietly for a few minutes and listen for His guidance.

Open the Eyes of My Heart
by Michael W. Smith

My Dear Jesus,

I have come this far in my effort to come closer to You, and I will not stop now. Give me courage and strength to continue on this journey in glorifying You. Open my heart to discern Your will for me in this process.

I praise You and give thanks to You for Your continual presence with me. May I take the time to recognize Your presence with me in all situations.

Day 61

The Jesus Prayer

Prayer of the Heart
Breath Prayer: A prayer that can be said in one breath.

The story is told in a Russian Spiritual Book called "The Way Of The Pilgrim"[151] of a poor Russian peasant traveling all over Russia and Siberia with only a knapsack, dried bread, a Bible, and a yearning to discover what the apostle Paul meant when he wrote in 1 Thessalonians 5.17, "Pray continually."

One day the pilgrim met a starets, a spiritual father, who taught him the Jesus Prayer: "Lord Jesus Christ, Son of God, have mercy on me." The spiritual father told him to pray it 3,000 times a day. After the pilgrim obliged, the spiritual father told him to do it 6,000 times a day, then 12,000. Eventually, the pilgrim stopped counting because the prayer had become a part of him, and he prayed it with every breath. . . he prayed continually![152]

You may make the Jesus Prayer more confessional by adding "a sinner" at the end. If you would like to make the prayer more communal, change the words to "have mercy on **us**."

The origin of the Jesus Prayer is most likely the Egyptian desert settled by the monastic Desert Fathers, monks living in the desert of Egypt in the 5th century.

The root of this prayer revolves around St. Paul's plea to the new believers of Thessalonica "to pray continually" (1 Thessalonians 5.17), In fact, Paul walked the talk; he practiced what he preached. "We also thank God continually" (1 Thessalonians 2.13), and the assurance he gave Timothy, "I constantly remember you in my prayers" (2 Timothy 1.3). In fact, whenever Paul speaks of prayer in his letters, two Greek words repeatedly appear: *pantote* (which means always); and *adialeptos* (meaning without interruption or unceasingly). Prayer is then not merely a part of life you can conveniently lay aside if something you deem more important comes up; prayer is all of life.[153]

The words of the Jesus Prayer are themselves based on Scriptural texts:

The cry of the blind man sitting by the roadside begging near Jericho, "Jesus, Son of David, have mercy on me!" (Luke 18.38).

The ten men who had leprosy that stood at a distance and called out, "Jesus, Master, have pity on us!" (Luke 17.13).

The cry of the tax collector at the temple, "God, have mercy on me a sinner" (Luke 18.13).

As you begin saying the Jesus Prayer, you are simply reciting the phrase verbally as an oral prayer. Later, you enter more deeply into the prayer in which you begin to say the prayer from your mind without distraction. Finally, in time, the prayer comes from the heart. You are saying the prayer without even thinking about it (thus, The Prayer of the Heart).

**"Lord Jesus Christ, Son of God,
have mercy on me, a sinner"**

Note to self

_____
_____
_____
_____
_____
_____
_____
_____
_____
_____

Day __62__

The Bearpaw Prayer
+ Other Breath Prayers

I also like the Scripture before and after "pray continually." 1 Thessalonians 5.16-17-18 says, "**Be joyful always**; pray continually; **give thanks in all circumstances**, for this is God's will for you." So I adapted the Jesus Prayer to my own breath prayer which focuses more on thanksgiving rather than confession.

**Father God,
thank you
for your love
and your presence
with me,
today and always.**

How often	1 Thess. 5.17	"Pray continually."
Father	1 John 3.1	"that we should be called children of God!"
Father	Genesis 1.27	"God created man in his own image."
God	Exodus 20.2	"I am the Lord your God."
Thank you	1 Thess 5.18	"Give thanks in all circumstances."

Love	Romans 8.38	"Neither height nor depth, nor anything else in all creation, will will be able to separate us from the love of God."
Presence	Leviticus 26.12	"I will walk among you and be your God."
Presence	Genesis 28.15	"I am with you and will watch over you wherever you go."
Today/ always	Matthew 28.20	"and surely, I am with you always."

Another way to recite Breath Prayers is to say the prayer slowly and meditate on each word and the Scripture it derived from. . . a form of Lectio Divina Prayer.

Breath Prayers are limited only to your creativity and the situation at the moment you create it. Following are samples and ideas of Breath Prayers:

Help, Father.
O Lord, fill me with Your love.
Heavenly Father, grant me Your grace.
Jesus, make me more like You.
O God, show me Your will for me.
Give me peace, O Lord.
Lord, forgive me.
Lord, change me.
I trust You, Jesus.
O Lord,. . . . .

> REMEMBER, Breath Prayers
> may also be used with prayer beads (Day 50).

Note to self

_____
_____
_____
_____
_____

Day 63

Let's Eat

M any Christians offer a prayer to God before each meal. I hope that you do, but if not I encourage you to begin! The options for meal-time prayers are endless. Some people offer an impromptu prayer stressing the relevance of the day, the activity of the time, the relationship to Scripture, or needs at the time. Thanksgiving is always appropriate, whether for the food available to you, for your life in general, or BOTH.

Others, however, offer a memorized prayer before each meal. My wife and I usually say a memorized prayer, unless moved by activities or events of the day to offer an impromptu prayer. We try to create a new "memorized" prayer every year or so to prevent us from "just saying" the prayer. Everyone is different. Pray in the way the Spirit moves you at the time.

"OKAY, I'll give prayers before meals at home a try, but I'm not going to pray at restaurants!" WHAT. . . . Did you really say that? Are you saying that you are too embarrassed to pray in places someone else might see you? We are going to address praying in public later in this book, but for now let's discuss the simple act of praying before meals, and let's focus on just you and/or your family. Again, you may choose an impromptu prayer or a memorized prayer. Until you feel confident about your prayers, you may want to keep the prayer short. (Heaven forbid, that someone might think you believe in God). But, also, to quote Jesus, "When you pray, do not keep on babbling like pagans, for they think they will be heard because of their many words" (Matthew 6.7). Remember, your objective is to praise, glorify, and thank God; asking him to bless your food and your service to Him. If you are "dragging out" the prayer just for length – you are missing the point. Go for it, you can do it!

PRAYERS FOR MEALS
(for your use or modification):

Almighty God, you have given your only son to be for us a sacrifice for sin, and also an example of Godly life; Give us grace to receive thankfully the fruits of His redeeming work, and to follow daily in the blessed steps of His most holy life; through Jesus Christ our Lord. Amen.

Bless us, O Lord for these Thy gifts which we are about to receive from Thy bounty, through Christ, our Lord. Amen. (traditional Catholic prayer)

Bless O Lord, this food to our use, and us to Thy loving service; and make us ever mindful of the needs of others, for Jesus' sake. Amen.

O Lord, we pray Thy blessings upon this food and upon our lives. Guide us through life and save us through Christ. Amen.

O Lord, with five loaves and two fish you fed and blessed thousands. We ask now your blessing upon this food and upon our lives. In Your name we pray. Amen.

Oh Thou who clothest the lilies and feedest the birds of the sky,
   Who leadest the lambs to pasture and the hart to the waterside.
   Who hast multiplied loaves and fishes and converted water to wine,
   Do Thou come to our table as Guest and Giver to dine.

Create your own meal-time prayer:
_____
_____
_____
_____

Day 64

How Long to Pray

Nice Segway! Yesterday we talked about the reason for keeping prayers short, but did Jesus really mean that when we are praying in our private room?

Let's hear from some notables about how long your prayer time should be.

Time spent in prayer is not time wasted, but time invested.[154] Don't feel guilty about spending time with God. It may be the most important "time" of your day. I truly hope you get to the point where you are saddened when you miss a day of prayer.

Jesus asked His disciples, "Could you not keep watch for one hour" (Matthew 14.37)? The very next statement is, "watch and pray" (Matthew 14.38), confirming that He was expecting the disciples to pray at least an hour.

Much time spent in prayer is the secret of all successful prayer. Your short prayers owe their point and efficiency to the long ones that have preceded them.[155]

Martin Luther (1483-1546), a German priest and scholar whose questioning of certain church practices led to the Protestant Reformation, said, "The fewer the words, the better the prayer." However, he has also been quoted as saying, "If I fail to spend two hours in prayer each morning, the devil gets the victory."

New Testament scholar Dom John Chapman (1865-1933), [Dom is a title given to certain monks and clerics] often quoted the following advice, "Pray as you can, not as you can't." If you cannot

144

pray for an hour, pray for whatever length of time you can. The point is, don't bail on Jesus using the excuse "I don't have time."

Your prayer time should not be measured by the clock, but it is important for you to know that spending lengthy, quality time with God is vital to your prayer. Take as much time to speak to Him as you need without rushing "just to get some time in." Be honest, sincere, and genuine as you talk to Him. When you have spoken your piece, sit quietly and "listen to Him" for a few minutes before closing. If this process takes 10 minutes or 60 minutes, your Father will say, "Well done, good and faithful servant!" (Matthew 25.21) if you indeed were speaking from your heart. Don't have the clock rule your prayer time. Instead have the Spirit control the amount of time you spend in prayer.

But remember, the quick instant prayers or short three-minute prayers are also valuable throughout the day. These prayers are important in keeping constant and continual communication with God. But, also make every effort you can to spend private, uninterrupted time with Him each day to sustain your intimate relationship with your Father.

A.S.A.P.

Always **S**ay **A P**rayer

Lord Jesus,

I truly desire to spend quality time with You. Sometimes I devote myself entirely to You, but other times I allow the world to take over my time. Be with me each day as I come to You, giving me the assurance that the time I spend with You is the most simple and basic way I can worship and love You.

Day 65

Trust Me

Trust = Faith

In her book <u>Jesus Calling</u>, Sarah Young asks you to learn a new habit. Try saying "I trust You, Jesus" in response to whatever happens to you.[156] This is yet another form of continual prayer, bringing your focus to Jesus and His control over the universe.

Many things may feel out of control. Your routines are not running smoothly. When you are shaken out of your comfort zone, grip God's hand tightly and look for growth opportunities. Say yes to His work in your life. Trust Him, and don't be afraid. When you give your trust totally to God, there is no limit as to how much He can strengthen you.[157]

Faith is actively trusting that God can handle your troubles and needs better than you can.[158] Faith is believing that God is present when all you hear is silence.[159]

Prayer is not some kind of heavenly lottery. Nor does the Bible counsel us to pray with an "I hope this will work" kind of attitude. Instead, we are told that prayer brings us before the throne of grace as children seeking the help of their heavenly Father.[160]

"Faith comes from hearing the message, and the message is heard through the Word of Christ" (Romans 10.17). The message, the Word of God, talks a lot about having faith in Him. Jesus says that your prayer must be combined with faith to be answered. "If you believe, you will receive whatever you ask for in prayer" (Matthew 21.22). We all too often read His Word, but fail to really believe He can do what He says.

> Faith is not believing God can do something,
> But that God **will** do something!

Prayer is absolutely dependent on faith. While faith does not bring the blessing, it puts prayer in a position to ask for it.[161] Genuine, authentic faith must be free of doubt. For if you pray with the pretense that nothing will happen, that God can't or won't answer your request, you are merely hoping for His favor instead of truly trusting His reply. No faith almost always means no answer. And honestly, why would you pray to God seeking his ultimate power if you did not believe in Him?

Hebrews Chapter 11 is often called "the faith chapter", or "God's Hall of Fame", or "the Hall of Faith." These men and women had immense faith that God would "provide" and thus trusted Him with their lives. And in so doing, God used these people in extraordinary ways. In the Gospel of Matthew alone, Jesus talks much about faith:

"Some men brought to him a paralytic, lying on a mat. When Jesus saw their faith,. . . (he healed the man)" (Matthew 9.2).

"Immediately Jesus reached out his hand and caught him (Peter). 'You of little faith,' He said, 'why did you doubt'" (Matthew 14.31)?

"I tell you the truth, if you have faith as small as a mustard seed, you can say to this mountain, 'move from here to there' and it will move. Nothing will be impossible for you" (Matthew 17.20).

"I tell you the truth, if you have faith and do not doubt. . . ." (Matthew 21.21).

So, it really goes back to the beginning of this day. Trust Jesus with all your heart. When you are weary and everything seems to go wrong, you can still utter these four words, "I trust You, Jesus."

 Blessings by Laura Story

"The only thing that counts is faith expressing itself through love" (Galatians 5.6).

Day 66

God Is With You

Too often we fail to remember that our loving God is with us every minute of every day. Sadly, we only think of Him when we are troubled and need help. Far too often we fail to see His face with us in all circumstances and certainly we fail to offer our thanks to Him throughout the day. Do you believe? Do you have faith that Jesus will keep His word? Read the following and realize that He is with you now and forever; He will NEVER leave you.

The last words Jesus spoke before ascending to heaven were, "I am with you always" (Matthew 28.20).

"I am with you and will watch over you wherever you go" (Genesis 28.15).

"Never will I leave you, never will I forsake you" (Hebrews 13.5).

"God will be with you wherever you go" (Joshua 1.9).

Do you fail to recognize God's presence? Are you too busy to recognize Him? Is Satan distracting you? Are you just ignoring Him? God IS with you 24/7. Remind yourself every day, no, every minute, every second that, "He will never leave you. He will never forsake you" (Hebrews 13:5). As you go through the day, keep in mind His holy presence with you. He has promised to be with you and to take care of you, if only you will believe Him, trust Him, and have faith in Him. He is always with you, so don't be afraid. He never leaves your side, He never lets go of your hand. "I am holding you by your right hand" (paraphrase Psalm 73.23). "I have made you and I will carry you" (Isaiah 46.4).

F.R.O.G.

Forever Rely On God

Think about this popular poem for a few minutes, then listen to Leona Lewis sing it – powerful!

The Footprints Prayer

One night I had a dream. . .

I dreamed I was walking along the beach with the Lord, and
Across the sky flashed scenes from my life.
For each scene I noticed two sets of footprints in the sand;
One belonged to me, and the other to the Lord.
When the last scene of my life flashed before us,
I looked back at the footprints in the sand.
I noticed that many times along the path of my life,
There was only one set of footprints.

I also noticed that it happened at the very lowest
and saddest times in my life
This really bothered me, and I questioned the Lord about it.
"Lord, you said that once I decided to follow you,
You would walk with me all the way;
But I have noticed that during the
most troublesome times in my life,
There is only one set of footprints.
I don't understand why in times when I
needed you the most, you should leave me.

The Lord replied, "My precious, precious
child. I love you, and I would never,
never leave you during your times of
trial and suffering.
When you saw only one set of footprints,
It was then that I carried you.

By Mary Stevenson © 1984 from original 1936 text

Footprints In The Sand by Leona Lewis

Day 67

Fasting

F asting is your intentional abstinence from eating. But, why would you do that?

A Christian fast is accompanied by a special focus on prayer during the fast. Your time of fasting is set apart to come closer to Christ. It is a means of giving up something of pleasure in order to devote your whole heart to God in prayer. You are simply putting all of your attention on God![162] Fasting does not change God; it changes you. When you fast, that is the appropriate time to be in prayer, not as a replacement for your normal prayers, but as an additional time of prayer.[163]

But is fasting really a good idea? The discipline of fasting may be dangerous if you are susceptible to eating disorders such as anorexia or bulimia. As with any food or exercise related activity, speak with your doctor if you have ANY questions. The Bible says often that you should fast. In the days of Jesus, Jews were required to fast on the Day of Atonement, but many fasted on a regular voluntary basis. The Pharisees fasted twice a week, on Mondays and Thursdays. Jesus gave the basic guidelines for fasting immediately after He explained "how to pray" in Matthew's gospel. "When you fast, do not look somber as the hypocrites do, for they disfigure their faces to show men they are fasting. I tell you the truth, they have received their reward in full. But when you fast, put oil on your head and wash your face, so that it will not be obvious to men that you are fasting, but only to your Father, who is in unseen; and your Father, who sees what is done in secret, will reward you" (Matthew 6.16-18). Like offering prayer, in this passage, Jesus is giving the expectation that you should fast. And like prayer, Jesus is saying your fast should not be done to make yourself appear as someone special. Jesus is ultimately saying that your fast should be between Him and you. Isaiah 58 warns against misguided fasting, when the true purpose of fasting is lost and it becomes a religious duty, causing pride and self-importance.[164] But if you approach fasting as an opportunity to enhance your prayer time, it is an awesome discipline. Time after time in the Bible, God's faithful spend time in fasting and prayer before a major decision or event in their lives.[165]

If you choose to try fasting as part of your spiritual life, there are some basic things to consider:

1. How long will your fast last? The duration of your fast may last from several hours to as long as 40 days.[166]
2. How often will you fast? Most people I know that fast do so once per week. For example, they may fast every Wednesday (either for the lunch meal or all day).
3. Can you plan for time of prayer during the time you would normally be eating?
4. Remember the purpose of fasting is directing your heart toward God, not to impress others of how pious you are.

Listed below are 50 passages of Scripture that relate to fasting. I encourage you to read these Scriptures before beginning a fasting discipline:

Matthew 6.16-18	Isaiah 58.3-7	Psalm 69.10	Joel 2.12	Luke 18.12
Nehemiah 1.4	Luke 4.2	Acts 13.3	Matthew 4.2	Esther 4.16
Ezra 8.21-23	Luke 2.37	Judges 20.26	Isaiah 58.6-7	Jonah 3.5-10
Daniel 10.2-3	Zechariah 8.19	Joel 1.14	Mark 2.18	Matthew 9.15
Nehemiah 9.1	Psalm 109.24	1 Samuel 31.13	Exodus 34.28-29	2 Samuel 1.12
Jeremiah 14.12	Esther 4.3	1 Chron. 10.12	Joel 2.15	Mark 1.13
2 Samuel 12.16	Daniel 6.18	Jeremiah 36.9	2 Chron. 20.3	Deut. 9.9-18
Lev. 23.26-32	Luke 5.33-35	1 Kings 21.27	Acts 27.23	1 Samuel 7.6
Acts 14.23	Psalm 35.13	Daniel 9.3	Zechariah 7.5	Acts 13.2
1 Kings 19.8	2 Samuel 3.35	Acts 9.9	Ezra 10.6	Mathew 4.4

Day 68

Did You Hear That?

A man once asked God why he never hears God speak to him, and God replied "because you do all of the talking." Communication and relationship with God is a two-way street. The only way you are going to hear God is if you take the time to listen to Him. Can you imagine how frustrating it must be for God to hear you ask, beg, plead, and carry on about your concerns when He knows them better than you yourself do; and yet you hardly ever listen to His response? I bet you already know this, but in a relationship you don't get to do all the talking! The same applies in your relationship with your heavenly Father. There comes a time when you simply have to sit quietly and listen in responsive silence for what the still, small voice might be whispering. Remember, quiet time with God is still communication. And, sometimes listening to God is even better than doing all of the talking.

Are you so occupied with your daily routines of work, television, internet, social media, and whatever else you can work into your life that you fail to listen to your Creator, your Father – Abba? Staying focused during your prayer time is difficult; it requires a lot of discipline. And, to remain silent after your prayers to listen to God is especially difficult. Your mind often tends to wander to far off places. When this happens, simply bring yourself back to God until your time of listening has completed.

You may also set aside a separate time of listening to God – time where you allow God, through the Holy Spirit, to lead the conversation. Again, start out with a short amount of time (maybe

3-5 minutes) and expand the time as you feel the calling. If you don't hear God speak to you, it is okay – you probably won't have a revelation every day; just relax and enjoy His company and know HE IS WITH YOU!

> Sit quietly and simply say, "Now Lord, I invite You to speak to me through Your Holy Spirit!"[167]

I have never seen God or audibly heard His voice, but I do talk with Him daily. Though I have witnessed no theophany (visible appearance of God), He has communicated with me many times through my thoughts, reading Scripture, and ideas (like this book). One of the things I personally have to work on and accept is the fear of silence. I suspect many of you also have this phobia. Let's both turn this over to God and ask Him to give us the courage to quietly listen.

If you want to hear God's voice, you must be willing to hear Him whenever and wherever He speaks. It most assuredly will not always be during your time of individual prayer, although that may be the time He touches you. You must be open and prepared to hear His voice at any time.

One place that you may be hearing God speak and not even realizing it is when reading the Bible. "In the beginning was the Word, and the Word was with God, and the Word was God" (John 1.1). "All Scripture is God-breathed and is useful for teaching, rebuking, correcting and training in righteousness" (2 Timothy 3.16). As you read the Bible, listen – don't just read. Then be willing to accept His Word and His calling for your response. In other words, don't ask God to speak to you if you don't want to hear His response. "Here I am! I stand at the door and knock. If anyone hears my voice and opens the door, I will come in and eat with him, and he with me" (Revelation 3.20).

Prayer of Mother Teresa

Dear Jesus, help me to spread Thy fragrance everywhere I go. Flood my soul with Thy Spirit and love. Penetrate and possess my whole being so utterly that all my life may only be a radiance of Thine. Shine through me and be so in me that every soul I come in contact with may feel Thy presence in my soul. Let them look up and see no longer me but only Jesus. Stay with me and then shall I begin to shine, so to shine as to be a light for others.

Day 69

Recalculating

Sometimes you might get "off-track" or you are taking the wrong path. It happens; you are human. You very well may rely on your own knowledge and compass to lead you in the right direction. "Recalculating. . . . . Make an immediate U-turn." Ever heard these words? If you have a GPS navigation system in your vehicle, I am sure you have heard them as the GPS unit warns you of your direction, and you usually correct your mistake.

But did you know there is another Navigation System available to you? Of course you did, and you know that God is the ultimate source of wisdom and direction (and **up** is the only direction that really counts). If you will only listen (go back to yesterday), God will lead **you** to Him. It may come to you through the gentle words of God reminding you that you are heading down the wrong path. He may warn you through His Word – Scripture; He may tell you through a song you hear; it may be something a friend says; or. . . He may softly bring you back on course as you quietly listen to Him in prayer.

God wants only the best for you, but He will allow you to make your own decisions and yes. . . . mistakes. But know this; "He is with you and will watch over you wherever you go" (Genesis 28.15). So where is your compass pointing?

The Holy Bible is truly an instruction book for you. It will provide you the answer to any question you may have, if you only read deep enough and study what the Word actually says.

"Teach me your way, O Lord, and I will walk in your truth" (Psalm 86.11).

"I will instruct and teach you in the way you should go" (Psalm 32.8).

"Man does not live by bread alone, but on every word that comes from the mouth of God" (Matthew 4.4).

"Reflect on what I am saying, for the Lord will give you insight into all this" (2 Timothy 2.7).

"For the Lord your God will be with you wherever you go" (Joshua 1.9).

"Then you will know the truth, and the truth shall set you free" (John 8.32)

Thy Word Is A Lamp Unto My Feet
by Maranatha! Singers

Are you off track? If so. . . RECALCULATE!

Note to self

_____

_____

_____

_____

_____

Day 70

Unanswered Prayer?

S orry, that just won't happen. There can be no question that
God wants you to pray and that He promises to answer your
questions. When you pray to God, you can be assured He hears
you and He will answer you. However, the answer you get may not
be the answer you want, but whatever the answer – it will be good,
for it is always in your best interest. You can be assured of that by
reading these Scriptures:

"I call on you, O God, for you will answer me" (Psalm 17.6).

"Ask and it shall be given to you. . ." (Matthew 7.7).

"For where two or three come together in my name, there I am
with them" (Matthew 18.20)

"If you believe, you will receive whatever you ask for in prayer"
(Matthew 21.22).

"You may ask me for anything in my name, and I will do it"
(John 14.14).

"If we ask anything according to His will, He hears us"
(1 John 5.14).

"Whatever you ask for in prayer, believe that you have
received it, and it will be yours" (Mark 11.24).

"My Father will give you whatever you ask in my name"
(John 16.23).

Garth Brooks, popular country singer, wrote a song in 1990
called <u>Unanswered Prayers</u>. The chorus of that song went like this:

"Sometimes I thank God for unanswered prayers
Remember when you're talking to the man upstairs
That just because He doesn't answer
doesn't mean He don't care
Some of God's greatest gifts are unanswered prayers."

You may sometimes become impatient in your prayer life. You might get angry and throw up your hands and decide God is not listening to you when He doesn't answer your prayers immediately or in the exact way you had hoped. But He will always answer in one of these five ways:[168]

1.   NO, I love you too much.
2.   Yes, but you will have to wait.
3.   Yes, but not exactly what you expected.
4.   Yes, I thought you would never ask.
5.   Yes, and here is more!

So, it is easy to see why you may think God is not answering your prayer. . . because His answer is not in "your time" or what you wanted. The problem with what you call "unanswered prayer" does not rest with God but with you. Most of your rejected prayers or delay in response come from the same Scripture verses stated earlier ("ask in my name," "ask according to His will," "if you believe"). Go back to Day 34 and review the hindrances to prayer.

Faith in God
includes faith
in His timing

Day 71

Praying Out Loud

Do what? Who me??
Are you crazy???

I can just hear you now. "Hold on there pal, you said in Day 17 that Jesus said to go into your room, close the door, and pray. That doesn't sound very much like praying in front of other people." OKAY, good point, you're right, but you are also told to pray continually. Unless you live in your "private room," you will have to pray in public places at some time. Factually, the Bible does not say that we should not pray in public. One of the "key factors" Jesus is talking about in Matthew 6.5-8 is **how** you pray. He was pointing out that the Pharisees prayed where they could be seen – really they were praying for other men. Luke 18.9-14 tells of the story of the Pharisee and the tax collector. Both men prayed out loud and in public. The tax collector prayed earnestly to God and was justified; the Pharisee prayed to himself and was not. Jesus wants your prayer to be sincere and from your heart. The best way to assure that you are not praying for other people to see is to pray in your "room", in secret.

In my opinion Jesus does not care if you pray in public places, even in front of many other people, if in fact you are praying with the right motive – and that is to glorify God. So with that philosophy in mind, let's look at why some people are so "afraid" to pray in public.

At some point, you will probably be asked to lead a prayer for a group of some kind. It may be in the church at a Sunday School

Class, prayer meeting, before a pot-luck, or a worship meeting. It could be outside of church at your men's Bible Study Meeting, at your house when you have guests over for dinner, or simply your turn at some sort of gathering. It could be that one group asks you to pray as a matter of personal growth for each person in the group – and yet another group may ask you to pray because they "cannot" (meaning they have less confidence than you). Regardless of the reason, do not turn down the opportunity; don't deny your Lord in public.

You may be shy or feel awkward when praying in front of other people. You may feel that others are better equipped to pray because of their Biblical knowledge or experience in prayer. But understand that God is not looking for eloquence of speech or "just the right words." He simply wants a faithful and honest heart. Your job is to pray in honesty; God's job is to listen and answer. Have faith that He will do His part, and your part becomes much easier.

In watching others and listening to comments about praying in public, I am convinced the number one reason for reluctance is a lack of confidence. I totally understand – been there, done that. This is not only true for praying in public but just about any other "activity" you have to "perform" in front of other people. As you know, you begin to feel better and better (more confident) each time you complete the activity. So enter into public prayer with the confidence that God is with you. Ask Him to provide the words for you to say. And, as you pray more in your "private" setting you will become more confident in praying with others. Have faith!

Here are a few simple suggestions for praying out loud:

1. Remember you are talking to God, not the people around you.
2. If you have time, practice in advance.
3. Praying with a family member or friend is a good starting point.
4. Be yourself. Talk like you would normally talk.
5. Share what is on your heart.
6. Keep it short and simple.

> Lord, may I be filled with faith and trust that when I pray in public I may always do so to honor and glorify you. As I reach out to pray with and for others, give me confidence in knowing that with You, nothing is impossible (Luke 1.37).

Day 72

Technical Support

Don't think for a minute that you are alone in this prayer process or that you don't have anyone to turn to for help or answers to questions. Besides a loving and caring heavenly Father who wants desperately to have you come closer to Him, in today's world there are thousands of resources available to answer almost any question you may have about prayer. Obviously, there is no way to record all of them (even if I wanted to), but I would like to throw out some ideas for your consideration.

First, let's explore the ever popular smart phone. I have no business trying to explain this gadget to you, because I am of an older generation with limited experience. I do, however, know these mini-computers have a lot to offer. (Did you know you can actually talk to someone without having a cord attached to the phone?) Besides internet capabilities, which will be discussed soon, most phone plans allow for the use of "apps". Some of my favorite apps are the Holy Bible (in several translations), eVotions (daily devotions sent to your phone each day), how to pronounce words in the Bible (awesome), prayer wall (a site where you can choose to pray for others around the world), and iTunes which has over 150 apps to support a Christian life.

The internet has made "going to the library" an at home experience. Again, I don't need to tell you how much information is available for your access at the push of a button. Whether you have a desk top computer, a tablet, or a smart phone, the internet and instant information is available at your convenience.

I encourage you to delve deeper into many and any of the topics discussed in this 90 day devotional, and those questions that arise from it. Be assured that I am not the final resource available to you about prayer.

A couple of prayer related activities you may want to look at on-line are:

1. International Day of Prayer (idop.org)
2. Anglican Fellowship of Prayer (afp.org)
3. Global Day of Prayer (globaldayofprayer.com)
4. National Day of Prayer (nationaldayofprayer.org)
5. Share prayers and pray for others (prayernetwork.org)
6. Worldwide prayer intercessors (internationalprayernetwork.com)
7. Prayer in general (prayernetwork.org)
8. America Praying On-line (apol.org)
9. Worldwide Prayer Chain (victorious.org/prayer)
10. The Book of Common Prayer (bcponline.org)

Of course music is available through any of the smart phones, tablets, or desk tops. For those with Sirius or another provider, Christian music is available via satellite in your vehicle – the same is true for satellite television subscribers. My wife and I listen to Christian music through all of the "channels".

I have not forgotten the use of Daily Devotionals. These will be discussed in more detail on Day 75.

Day 73

Journaling

P rayer is almost always done orally, but it doesn't have to be. In fact, you may find that writing down your prayers enables you to communicate with God at a deeper level than you can with spoken prayer. This discipline is commonly known as journaling.[169]

A prayer journal contains thoughts arising from prayer. Your thoughts may be of thanksgiving, penitence, humor, confession, fear, or anger at God. Hold nothing back, for God knows it all before you write it down. Be completely honest in what you write and let your words flow with no boundaries.[170] The discipline of journaling provides a natural method of recording how God is working in your life at the time a certain event happens.[171] In short, journaling is similar to keeping a daily diary. The use of pen and paper are still very popular today. However, many find the technology of a computer or tablet much more appealing.

Using a prayer journal may have different implications to each of you. Some may view this as a daily interjection with a lot of verbiage and thoughts recorded. You may choose to write your prayers and requests instead of saying them orally. Most likely you would write down what you feel God is speaking back to you.

Another option for consideration in the use of a journal is to use it as a guideline for your prayers. The varieties of use vary as much as there are people. Everyone has their own ideas as to how this journal might help them come closer to Christ. I personally don't keep a prayer "journal", but instead keep a prayer "notebook" with my requests and answers recorded. You can refer back to Day 26 for a sample of how I set up my prayer (journal).

Remember, there are no rules, so use the journal in a way that improves your communication with Christ. As with your personal prayer time, you may also discover the use of a journal and the way it is used may change as you "change" or mature in your relationship with god. The important thing to remember is that the journal is for you. Experiment with it; do whatever works best for you.

In using a journal, you should feel free and comfortable in writing exactly and honestly what is on your mind. What is written in the journal stays in the journal. When you write your prayers down, you may put some of your innermost, private thoughts and secrets down on paper.[172] If you choose to share your journal with someone, that is your choice. Otherwise your journal is off limits—between you and God only.

Keeping a journal over the years becomes a great way to see where you have come from spiritually. Thus, as you could imagine, it is important to record the date (including the year) with each entry you make.

This style of prayer is not my forte'. I can see the value and potential of it, but I just personally do not use it. So, I encourage you to get more information about it by searching your computer under "prayer journal".

Note to self

_____
_____
_____
_____
_____
_____
_____
_____
_____
_____
_____
_____
_____
_____
_____

Day 74

A Note to God

W hen moved by the Holy Spirit, use your journaling time or quiet time to write God a letter, poem, or song. This is an opportunity for you to express your thoughts, feelings, and love for Him. Indeed, it is yet another form of worship.

By keeping your "note" on a computer file or flash drive, in a file cabinet, on your phone / tablet, or in your journal, you will be able to access and review your thoughts at a later date.

As I mentioned on Day 57, I have learned to play the guitar. What a joy this form of worship has added to my life! Although I am by no means a professional musician, I am moved to sing to our Lord, and occasionally put my own words to music. In 2010 my wife and I visited the Holy Land in Israel for ten days. What an awesome experience to walk and pray where Jesus spent His ministerial days on earth! Immediately after the trip, I was led by the Holy Spirit to write a song about my feelings. So be prepared for God to touch your heart – at any time! Following is a note I wrote to my Lord, printed only as an example of things you could do.

SONG OF HEAVEN
W/M BEARPAW 12.2012 Bearpaw Productions

This is the song we will sing in heaven; Holy, Holy, is the Lord!
In the light of His presence, We will all bow before Him;

CHORUS
This is the song of heaven. I can hardly wait to sing it;
Come let us gather, and share our meal with God;
Holy, Holy, is the Lord! Holy, Holy, is the Lord!
Selah after CHORUS (time of reflection; instrumental)
CODA: Repeat CHORUS

God takes away our tears and our fears; Holy, Holy, is the Lord!
Cherubim and seraphim, angels and I will boldly say;
CHORUS

Mar-anatha. Mar-anatha. Mar-anatha. Come O Lord!
Amen. Come, Lord Jesus Amen. Come, my Lord!
CHORUS

Rev 4.8: "Day and night they(seraphs) never stop saying
'Holy, holy, holy is the Lord God Almighty . . .'"
Isaiah 6.2: "Holy, holy, holy is the Lord God Almighty."
Rev 7.17: "God will wipe away every tear from their eyes."
(also Rev 21.4)
Rev 19.6: "Hallelujah! For our Lord God Almighty reigns."
Rev 19.17: "Come, gather together for the great supper of God."
Rev 22.20: "Amen. Come, Lord Jesus." (maranatha: Aramaic
for 'Come O Lord)
Psalm 95.6: "Come, let us bow down in worship, let us kneel
before the Lord our Maker."
Isaiah 45.23: "Before me every knee will bow." (also
Romans 14.11)
Cherubim & seraphim: heavenly beings whose primary pur-
pose is to worship God at His throne.

Day 75

Devotionals

Supplements to your reading.

Daily devotionals provide opportunities to discover what others have experienced on their walk with Christ and how Scripture relates to their story. These devotionals most often correlate a personal story by the author to the Words of Scripture. Reading these devotionals each day is very inspiring since you can usually "paint yourself into the picture." In addition, they provide suggested daily reading of Scripture, and most include some format of reading the Bible in a year.

Daily devotionals come in many formats, the three most common are:

Small Booklets published every month or two. The authors of these devotionals vary from individuals across America and the world to well-known pastors. Many local churches provide these to their congregations for free. Otherwise, you may make your own personal subscription via internet access as provided below.

Books which are published yearly. As you would expect, there is a devotional for every day of the year. There are hundreds of options and authors to choose from. Most of the authors are pastors or well-known authors of Christian Books. I have listed some of my favorites, but you can access amazon.com or visit your local bookstore for other ideas.

E-devotionals which can be sent to your computer or phone. Most of these are free. The author is usually a recognized pastor or author of Christian Books.

Yearly subscriptions or free:

Christ in Our Home	www.augsburgfortress.org
Men of Integrity	www.MenOfIntegrity.net
Forward Day By Day	www.forwardmovement.org
Upper Room	www.upperroom.org
Days of Praise	www.icr.org
Our Daily Bread	www.odb.org
Still Speaking	www.ucc.org
Words of Hope	www.woh.org
In Touch	www.intouch.org
Bible Gateway Daily Devotional	www.biblegateway.com
Prayer Today Daily Devotional	www.prayertoday.org
Prayer Central Daily Devotional	www.prayercentral.org/devotional

Some yearly devotional books I really like are:

James, Arthur. God Calling. Uhrichsville. Barbour Publishing, Inc. 1952

Wilkinson, Bruce. Closer Walk. Grand Rapids. Zondervan. 1992

Tiegreen, Chris. The One Year at His Feet Devotional. Carol Stream. Tyndale House Publishers, Inc. 2003

Tiegreen, Chris. The One Year Walk With God Devotional. Carol Stream. Tyndale House Publishers, Inc. 2004

Tiegreen, Chris. The One Year Worship the King Devotional. Carol Stream. Tyndale House Publishers, Inc. 2008

Lucado, Max. Grace for the Moment. Nashville. Thomas Nelson. 2007

Young. Sarah. Jesus Calling. Nashville. Thomas Nelson. 2004

Seybert. Jim. The One Year Mini Devotional for Leaders. Carol Stream. Tyndale House Publishers, Inc. 2007

Beers, Ronald; Beers, Gilbert. The One Year Mini for Women. Carol Stream. Tyndale House Publishers, Inc. 2005

Warren, Rick. <u>Daily Inspiration for The Purpose Driven Life</u>. Grand
   Rapids. Zondervan. 2004

I personally enjoy reading daily devotionals. (I currently read
five different devotional books each day). I hope you will consider
expanding your reading to include a daily devotional.

Day 76

Worship

A few years back someone sent me an email about worship that truly hit home. "A woman was seated in the congregation anxious for the service to begin – and end. She was already making a list of things to do as soon as church was over. Her heart just wasn't in tune with God's. As the service progressed, she became more and more critical. The music team was out of sync, she didn't like the song selection, the power-point operator was too slow in changing the words on the screen, the vocalists were off key, you name it and she criticized it. Finally, she said to the Lord, 'Lord, this music is not doing anything for me.' She then heard God reply softly to her heart, 'It's not for you.' "

How often do each of us do the same thing? Do you need to be reminded, "It's not about you?" Your time of worship needs to be spent glorifying and honoring God. You should praise Him for His unending love and grace, for the blessings He gives you though you are undeserving, and for His continual presence with you every minute of every day. You see, worship is to God and for God, not you.

Worship is not part of the Christian life, it is the Christian life.[173] Although cooperate worship in church on Sunday is vital, it is not the only time you can or should worship God. Worship is so much more than attending church with the Body of Christ. You also worship God in your daily life throughout the day by your offerings of love to others, respect, adoration, praise, service, music, and prayer.

In your growth of worship and service, regardless of what method it is, I pray that you develop beyond the "I have to" stage to the "I want to" and "I get to" stage. Going to church on Sunday should not be viewed as an obligation or as an event at which to be seen. It should be done in true honor and glory to God with thanksgiving that you have a loving Lord. So ask yourself, "Why do I go to church? Really. . . do I go to truly worship God? Do I go because I want to or because I feel obligated to? Do I worship God when I'm not in church?"

One of the easiest, clearest, and most profound ways to worship God is to talk about Him. You should tell others how He has been kind to you, the deeds He has done for you, and the blessings of His compassion that you have experienced. In short, you should give a testimony of God's love. Don't feel shy or intimidated; the glory of the Lord is worth more than the approval of man.[174]

 10,000 Reasons by Matt Redman

O Lord, open my heart and open my mind to not limit time of "worship" to Sunday morning only. As I become more and more aware of your continual presence with me, may I expand my worship of You through other avenues of worship. May You always be the center of my attention as I offer my praise, honor, and glory to You.

I hope worship becomes so much more than a weekly habit or routine.

Day 77

Father's Love Letter

Father's Love Letters is a compilation of Bible verses from both the Old and New Testaments that are presented in the form of a love letter from God to you.

Each line in the Father's Love Letters' message is paraphrased, which means each Scripture's overall message has been summarized into a simple phrase to best express its meaning. The words of this letter come from the heart of God, and so are true in every sense. What an awesome Father you have – one that loves you more than you could ever imagine!

Some of you may enjoy this message, others may not. I personally take it as a means to contemplate God's unending love and can visualize Him saying these words to me.

Read this message slowly. Take your time and really digest what it is saying to you. With our limited minds it is hard to imagine, but one thing I promise you, "Your Father in heaven does love you!" God's love for you isn't an obligation. It thrills Him.[175] He looks forward to your daily efforts to talk to Him. Enjoy His conversation back to you!

To view this letter in a powerful video presentation, connect to the following link: http://www.andiesisle.com/Love_Letter.html

*God
Loves
You*

The cry of a Father's heart from Genesis to Revelation...

Father's Love Letter

My Child...

You may not know me,
but I know everything about you... *Psalm 139:1*
I know when you sit down and when you rise up... *Psalm 139:2*
I am familiar with all your ways ... *Psalm 139:3*   Even the very hairs on your head are numbered... *Matthew 10:29-31*
For you were made in my image... *Genesis 1:27*   In me you live and move and have your being... *Acts 17:28*   For you
are my offspring... *Acts 17:28*   I knew you even before you were conceived... *Jeremiah 1:4-5*   I chose you when I
planned creation... *Ephesians 1:11-12*   You were not a mistake... *Psalm 139:15-16*   For all your days are written in my book
... *Psalm 139:15-16*   I determined the exact time of your birth and where you would live... *Acts 17:26*   You are fearfully
and wonderfully made... *Psalm 139:14*   I knit you together in your mother's womb... *Psalm 139:13*   And brought you
forth on the day you were born... *Psalm 71:6*   I have been misrepresented by those who don't know me... *John 8:41-44*
I am not distant and angry, but am the complete expression of love... *1 John 4:16*   And it is my desire to lavish
my love on you... *1 John 3:1*   Simply because you are my child and I am your Father... *1 John 3:1*   I offer you more
than your earthly father ever could... *Matthew 7:11*   For I am the perfect Father... *Matthew 5:48*   Every good gift that you
receive comes from my hand... *James 1:17*   For I am your provider and I meet all your needs... *Matthew 6:31-33*
My plan for your future has always been filled with hope... *Jeremiah 29:11*   Because I love you with an everlasting
love... *Jeremiah 31:3*   My thoughts toward you are countless as the sand on the seashore... *Psalm 139:17-18*   And I rejoice
over you with singing... *Zephaniah 3:17*   I will never stop doing good to you... *Jeremiah 32:40*   For you are my treasured
possession... *Exodus 19:5*   I desire to establish you with all my heart and all my soul... *Jeremiah 32:41*   And I want to
show you great and marvelous things... *Jeremiah 33:3*   If you seek me with all your heart, you will find me
... *Deuteronomy 4:29*   Delight in me and I will give you the desires of your heart ... *Psalm 37:4*   For it is I who gave you
those desires... *Philippians 2:13*   I am able to do more for you than you could possibly imagine... *Ephesians 3:20*   For I am
your greatest encourager... *2 Thessalonians 2:16-17*   I am also the Father who comforts you in all your troubles
... *2 Corinthians 1:3-4*   When you are brokenhearted, I am close to you... *Psalm 34:18*   As a shepherd carries a lamb, I have
carried you close to my heart... *Isaiah 40:11*   One day I will wipe away every tear from your eyes... *Revelation 21:3-4*
And I'll take away all the pain you have suffered on this earth... *Revelation 21:4*   I am your Father and I love you
even as I love my son, Jesus... *John 17:23*   For in Jesus my love for you is revealed ... *John 17:26*   He is the exact
representation of my being... *Hebrews 1:3*   And He came to demonstrate that I am for you, not against you
... *Romans 8:31*   And to tell you that I am not counting your sins... *2 Corinthians 5:18-19*   Jesus died so that you and I
could be reconciled... *2 Corinthians 5:18-19*   His death was the ultimate expression of my love for you... *1 John 4:10*
I gave up everything I loved that I might gain your love... *Romans 8:31-32*   If you receive the gift of my son Jesus,
you receive me... *1 John 2:23* And nothing will ever separate you from my love again... *Romans 8:38-39* Come home and
I'll throw the biggest party heaven has ever seen... *Luke 15:7*   I have always been Father and will always be
Father... *Ephesians 3:14-15*   My question is...Will you be my child?... *John 1:12-13*   I am waiting for you... *Luke 15:11-32*

...Love, Your Dad

Almighty God

Day 78

Scripted Prayers

Surely by now you have come to understand that there is no right or wrong way to pray. I hope you realize your heavenly Father only wants your heart and cares little about the exact words you say.

Some of you may prefer your thoughts and words to God be spontaneous and impromptu. You may want each day's prayers to be responsive to your feelings and emotions at the time.

Others, however, may feel most comfortable in reciting pre-written (scripted) prayers. These prayers may be found in any number of resources – one being The Book of Common Prayer. Christian bookstores usually have many choices of books available with scripted prayers for you to choose from. I know some people that offer prayers in public on a frequent basis that just don't feel comfortable presenting the requests "off-the-cuff". They usually write their prayer on a piece of paper, then read it. This is certainly an acceptable and good way to offer your requests without stumbling and mumbling, provided you have the time to write the prayer in advance. A common scripted prayer is the prayer said before meals (see Day 63). Certainly not always, but often these are short pre-written prayers.

And, of course, others—myself included, often offer prayers using both personal heart-felt prayers and pre-written prayers that fit the situation being prayed for.

Following are good examples of scripted, pre-written prayers[176]:

MORNING PRAYER

Thank you for the blessing for a new morning and the privilege of beginning the day by talking with You. I give You myself and my schedule today, asking to be used to further Your kingdom.

Grant me the wisdom to handle each situation I encounter with grace so that my speech will be pleasing and my thoughts pure as I follow Your direction. I am grateful that Your plans for me are good (Jeremiah 29.11), and I trust in Your steadfast faithfulness.

Help me to live in a manner worthy of the calling You have placed on my life (Ephesians 4.1) and to magnify Your name in all things.
Amen.

The Lord's loving kindnesses indeed never cease, for His compassions never fail. They are new every morning; great is your faithfulness (Lamentations 3.22-23).

EVENING PRAYER

As another day comes to an end, I am thankful for Your provision and protection, and I am humbled by the opportunity to experience Your constant presence.

I sought to glorify You in all I said and did today. Even as I sleep, I pray my thoughts will be focused on what honors You (Philippians 4.8). Let me wake in the morning refreshed and renewed with a heart yearning to serve.

Thank You for extending me Your wisdom and grace. I am grateful for Your unconditional love. How wonderful it is to abide in Your rest!
Amen.

I will bless the Lord who has counseled me; indeed, my mind instructs me in the night. I have set the Lord continually before me; because He is at my right hand, I will not be shaken (Psalm 16.7-8).

Day 79

Instant Prayers / Substitution Prayers

An extremely powerful, yet simple form of prayer is *instant prayers*. These prayers are usually very short and concise as you pray your thoughts and feelings to God. Your days are busy, but that is no excuse to discontinue your prayers. As you go through the tasks of the day, it is easy and simple, yet appropriate and reverent to say a five-second instant prayer to let God know you are thinking of Him and that He is in control of your life.

Your prayers do not have to be said aloud. Here is an example I found at www.svots.edu:

"A small group of high school students were visiting a home for unwed mothers. The woman who directed the home spoke to them for a half hour. Because the woman sensed the students were wondering about her faith commitment, she said, 'Well, you have been here thirty minutes, and I have prayed fifteen times.' She hadn't been out of their sight, nor out of their conversation. Yet, during the active interchange, this woman found the desire, attention, and time to offer instant prayers."

Think back to Days 61 and 62. . . The Jesus Prayer and The Bearpaw Prayer. If you get into the unconscious habit of constantly praying to and thinking about God, you will find that offering short instant prayers becomes not only easy, but natural. What a wonderful

180

opportunity to keep in touch with your heavenly Father and, at the same time offer your prayers of support and needs of others!

On day 44 we talked about praying through the use of Scripture. Here are some other ideas for using your Bible in unity with your prayers. You have discovered that by praying the words of Scripture, you are indeed praying God's own words. In so doing you can feel confident you are praying according to the will of God! By using Scripture you can read a passage and "substitute" words of that passage with the name(s) of the person(s) you are praying for.

As you regularly read your Bible you will probably come across many passages that will fit the needs of a "substitution" prayer. Below is a common passage that is used often in "substitution" prayers.

Colossian Prayer

As you pray the words of this passage, substitute the name of the person you are praying for each time you see a "you."

"For this reason, since the day we heard about you, we have not stopped praying for you and asking God to fill you with the knowledge of His will through all spiritual wisdom and under-standing. And we pray this in order that you may live a life worthy of the Lord and may please Him in every way; bearing fruit in every good work, growing in the knowledge of God, being strengthened with all power according to his glorious might so that you may have great endurance and patience, and joyfully giving thanks to the Father, who has qualified you to share in the inheritance of the saints in the kingdom of light" (Colossians 1.9-12).

Consider reading John 17.6-19 as a substitution prayer.

Note to self

_____
_____
_____
_____

Day 80

God or Jesus?

The question is sometimes asked, "Who do I pray to? Does it matter if I pray to God, or to Jesus, or to the Holy Spirit?"

Prayers in the Old Testament were obviously addressed to God the Father. The people of the day were awaiting the arrival of the Messiah, but Jesus had not been introduced yet.

Prayers of the New Testament have three options, depending on what stage of that section you are reading. The Gospels of Matthew, Mark, Luke, and John are primarily the Words of Jesus Christ. As such, most of the prayers were addressed to God the Father because most of the prayers were by Jesus. It would be really weird for Jesus to pray to himself (more on that later). Since Jesus was in constant prayer to God His Father, it appears that the answer has been given. You are to pray to God.

But—hold on. The remainder of the New Testament reveals the true Holy Trinity—God the Father, Son, and Holy Spirit—three persons in one. So in essence, if you are praying to God the Father, you are effectively praying to God that is Jesus and God that is the Holy Spirit also.

There is a lot of controversy about this question. There are many people much more qualified to answer this question than I am, but I firmly, 100% believe in the Holy Trinity and believe our God (all three persons) to be omnipotent (all powerful), omnipresent (present in all places), and omniscient (all knowing). I do not believe He cares which one of the three persons you pray to because they are all Him! I have the faith and confidence that

God is powerful enough to sort out our feeble insecurities and our need to be "right," and He will receive our request regardless of its recipient.

So let's take a look at Scripture related to the question of "who to pray to":

"Come, O Lord" (1 Corinthians 16.22). (Aramaic: Maranatha). This implies that prayers were addressed to the risen, glorified Christ. It verifies that Jesus was often referred to as Lord.

Jesus said, "You may ask for anything in my name, and I will do it" (John 14.14)

"If any of you lacks wisdom, he should ask God, who gives generously to all without finding fault, and it will be given to him" (James 1.5).

"Together with all those everywhere who call on the name of our Lord Jesus Christ" (1 Corinthians 1.2).

"Sing and make music in your heart to the Lord" (Ephesians 5.19).

"Repent of this wickedness and pray to the Lord" (Acts 8.22).

Thomas said to Jesus, "My Lord and my God" (John 20.28).

Jesus said, "My Father will give you whatever you ask in my name" (John 16.23).

"Then they prayed, Lord you know everyone's heart" (Acts 1.24).

What about the third person of the Holy Trinity – the Holy Spirit? We will discuss that tomorrow.

Day 81

The Holy Spirit
(our helper)

To me, the Bible teaches that you can pray to God – Father, Son, or Holy Spirit—because they are three in one, the same.

Our focus today is prayer to the Holy Spirit. Sometimes the Holy Spirit is forgotten about. It seems the Holy Spirit to some has become a "lesser" part of the triune. But be assured the Holy Spirit is an equal part of the Holy Trinity, and has an equal part in our life here on earth.

After rising from the dead, Jesus said to His disciples, "I am going to send you what my Father has promised; but stay in the city until you have been clothed with power from on high" (Luke 24.49).

Jesus also said, "Receive the Holy Spirit" (John 20.22).

It is obvious Jesus, even in His earthly form, was aware of the Holy Spirit and the power His equal had. He appeared anxious for this Spirit to arrive on earth and empower the believers with an invisible yet powerful source to believe in and pray to.

You are reminded what Paul told the Christians in Rome about a life through the Spirit, "In the same way, the Spirit helps us in our weakness. We do not know what we ought to pray for, but the Spirit Himself intercedes for us with groans that words cannot express" (Romans 8.26).

"But you dear friends, build yourselves up in your most holy faith and pray in the Holy Spirit" (Jude 20).

Many scripted prayers to the Holy Spirit have been written, one of which is below:

If you feel like you don't know how to pray. You have the wonderful promise that when you pray, the Holy Spirit intercedes for you according to the will of God.

I Asked God

I asked God to take away my pride. God said, "No. It is not for me to take away, but for you to give it up."

I asked God to make my handicapped child whole.
God said, "No. Her spirit is whole, her body is only temporary."

I asked God to grant me patience. God said, "No. Patience is a by-product of tribulations; it isn't granted, it is earned.

I asked God to give me happiness. God said, "No. I give You blessings, happiness is up to you."

I asked God to spare me pain. God said, "No. Suffering draws you apart from worldly cares and brings you closer to me."

I asked God to make my spirit grow. God said,
"No. You must grow on your own, but I will prune you to make you fruitful."

I asked God for all things that I may enjoy life.
God said, "No. I will give you life so that you may enjoy all things."

I asked God to help me LOVE others, as much as God loves me. God said. . . . "Ahhhhh. . . .finally you have the idea!"

Author Unknown

Day 82

Prayer vs. Satan

Satan knows that an individual or church is only as powerful as its prayer life, so he dreads nothing more than PRAYER. He will, therefore, make every attempt to keep you from praying. Some of his tactics may include:

He will tell you lies about God. . . . . (2 Corinthians 2.11)
   God doesn't love you.
   God is not going to come through for you.
   God can't forgive that.
   God's Word works for everyone but you.
   God doesn't care about you.

He will try to. . . . .
   Steal your prayer time and time in the Word.
   Wear down your enthusiasm.
   Interrupt your prayer time.
   Take your focus from God when praying.
   Tell you that you are not eloquent enough in speaking.
   Tell you that you don't have time to pray.

   Satan is not omnipotent (unlimited power or authority), omniscient (all knowing), or omnipresent (present in all places) – for only God the Almighty possesses all of these attributes, so how is it that Satan can be so powerful and attack so many? Although Satan is but one, he has in his power a vast army of fallen, evil spirits – demons who are evil, powerful, many in number, unclean, fallen angels (2 Peter 2.4). Demonology is clearly set forth in God's Word. They are intelligent (recognized Christ, Mark 1.24), they possess people (Matthew 8.29), they overcome men (Acts 19.13-16), they know their destiny (Matthew 8.29), they create error through lies (1 Timothy 4.1), they produce harm (Mark 5.1-5). They ultimately are assigned to cause prayerlessness.

Here are some words about Satan from various authors:

"Satan trembles when he sees even the weakest saint upon his knees" (William Cowder).

"When a Christian shuns fellowship with other Christians, the devil smiles. When he stops studying the Bible, the devil laughs. When he stops praying, the devil shouts for joy" (Corrie Ten Boom).

"The one concern of the devil is to keep Christians from praying. He fears nothing from prayerless studies, prayerless work, and prayerless religion. He laughs at our toil, mocks our wisdom, but trembles when we pray" (Samuel Chadwick).

"When the devil sees a man or woman who really believes in prayer, who knows how to pray, and who really does pray, and above all, when he sees a whole church on its face before God in prayer, he trembles as much as he ever did, for he knows that his day in that church or community is at an end" (R. A. Torrey).

"The primary way to overcome Satan is on our knees" (Derek Prime).

"Prayer is the master strategy that God gives for the defeat and rout of Satan" (Wesley L. Duewel).

Because of the sacrifice our Lord Jesus Christ made on the cross, Satan has been defeated. But know this, he will constantly and continually try to separate you from Christ. Be strong, be courageous, and withstand his temptations.

Day 83

Come, Follow Me!

J esus said at the Sea of Galilee to his two future disciples (Peter and Andrew), "Come, follow me" (Matthew 4.19). He also says the very, exact same thing to you and me. "I will make you fishers of men," He said. OKAY, that sounds good, count me in!

But, there is much more to following Jesus than merely tagging along and waiting for our meeting at the pearly gates. There is so much more than just going to church on Sunday morning, then forgetting about Him until the next Sunday. Jesus wants you to follow Him completely, to be His disciple. But the cost of being a disciple is not easy or cheap. Jesus said some very defining words to those traveling with Him, "If anyone comes to me and does not hate his father and mother, his wife and children, his brothers and sisters – yes, even his own life – he cannot be my disciple. And anyone who does not carry his cross and follow me cannot be my disciple" (Luke 14.25-27). Jesus is not asking you to "hate" your family, but rather to love them less than you do Him – to make Jesus the priority in your life. And by carrying His cross, you are willing to pay the full price for Him – to be crucified in His name. The cost to be a disciple and follow Jesus was immense. The Bible mentions only the deaths of two disciples, James who was put to death by Herod Agrippa in 44 AD (Acts 12.1-2) and Judas Iscariot who committed suicide shortly after the death of Jesus (Matthew 27.5). According to traditions, eight of the Apostles died as Martyrs, and at least two of them were crucified (Peter and Andrew).

Come, follow me! Do you still want to follow Him?

Jesus did not say, "Come follow me to church." He had much more in mind than that. So what does following Jesus require? First and foremost it is the full acceptance that Jesus Christ is Lord of all Lords, the Almighty. "If you confess with your mouth, 'Jesus is Lord,' and believe in your heart that God raised Him from the dead, you will be saved. For it is with your heart that you believe and are justified, and it is with your mouth that you confess and are saved" (Romans 10.9-10).

You are to follow Him in His Word. The only way to know the direction God intends for you to travel is to understand His Word. And, the only way to understand His Word is to read and study it. Then, the difficult task comes in applying His Word to your life. In having a better understanding of the Bible, you are preparing yourself to hear God's will and intent for you.

You are to follow Him by spreading the Good News. After Jesus rose from the dead, He met His disciples on a mountain in Galilee. He told them, "All authority in heaven and on earth has been given to me. Therefore go and make disciples of all nations, baptizing them in the name of the Father and of the Son and of the Holy Spirit, and teaching them to obey everything I have commanded you. And surely, I am with you always, to the very end of the age" (Matthew 28.18-20).

You are to follow Him in prayer. That was your original intent in reading this book, and it is an essential criterion in following your Lord. "Do not be anxious about anything, but in everything, by prayer and petition, with thanksgiving, present your requests to God. And the peace of God, which transcends all understanding, will guard your hearts and your minds in Christ Jesus" (Philippians 4.6-7). "Be joyful always, pray continually, give thanks in all circumstances, for this is God's will for you in Christ Jesus" (1 Thessalonians 5.16-18).

Come, follow me! From here to heaven.

Day __84__

Walk to Emmaus

I accepted Christ in 1969 at the age of 17. I had been attending church with my beautiful mother for the previous four years. All was good in my life, I even attended church each Sunday during my college days. After college, I married the love of my life, Debi. We had faithfully attended church every week for 30+ years and felt we were good Christian people.

Then, in 2005 I attended a 3-day Christian Retreat called Walk to Emmaus. . . . . and my life was changed! After spending 72 hours with 75 other Christian men, I realized how much I had been missing out on – and how much I had been cheating God. Among several other things, I made a commitment at the end of that retreat to start a real prayer life with my friend and Savior, Jesus Christ! Like you, I started this new, revitalized relationship with Christ with relatively brief conversations. But as time has gone by, I find myself spending more time than I ever imagined I would with Him – and wishing I would spend even more. You see, I too, am still growing closer to Christ. We all have to start somewhere.

Maybe you too, could benefit from and be interested in attending a Christian retreat. I am partial to the Walk to Emmaus because it is composed of an ecumenical group. The servants on the team and the "pilgrims" attending the walk all come from varied denominational backgrounds. But when it is all said and done, every person at the retreat realize they have the same belief and love for our wonderful God. Various denominations have similar weekends for their church denomination only. Talk to your pastor or priest about the possibilities in your area, or go to 3dayol.org for information about 3-day Christian retreats. If you are interested in the Walk to Emmaus, go to Emmaus.upperroom.org for more information.

Walk to Emmaus

The Walk to Emmaus is not actually a walk at all. You do not go hiking and make stops along the way to talk or pray. Instead, you remain in a conference room most of the time and hear various speakers talk about topics of Christian growth and their personal witness to support that topic. There is time for group and individual prayer, examination of personal practices, lots of praise and singing, and interaction with men or women of faith from other denominations. The goal of Walk to Emmaus is not to "find Christ", for it is encouraged that the participants already be Christians. The purpose of the walk is to bring all present closer to Christ and to encourage more participation in your local church and personal life. The theme of the weekend is Luke 24.13-35, on the road to Emmaus. Summary of this Scripture reveals two people walking from Jerusalem to the small village of Emmaus after the women and disciples had found the tomb of Jesus empty. As they were walking, Jesus came and started walking with them, although they did not recognize Him. As the three walked, Jesus explained to them all that was said in the Scriptures about Him. When they arrived at Emmaus, the two invited Jesus to stay with them. Jesus did, and when He was at the table with them He broke bread and shared it with them. Immediately the eyes of the two were opened and they recognized Jesus! They immediately ran back to Jerusalem to tell the others they had seen the risen Christ. And they told themselves, "Were not our hearts burning within us!"

So the Walk to Emmaus is not so much a "walk" as it is a journey with Christ in the hope of having your eyes opened and your heart set on fire!

Lord, open my heart to the possibility of attending a Christian retreat. What is Your will for me?

Day 85

Ever Thought About. . . . .?

There is certainly nothing wrong with sitting quietly in a chair, talking in any manner you wish to your sovereign God. But, your prayer life has many options. Have you ever thought about adding some creativity to your prayer time? Maybe you would like to add some ambience, some special features to the time you spend developing this relationship.

Candles and/or incense are common additions to the prayer room, especially at night or when the light is low. There is just something about a glowing candle, not to mention the fact that "fire" is a common symbol of the Holy Spirit.

Soft music playing in the background may offer you peace and tranquility. It may soothe your tensions and increase your focus on the privilege of praying to God. If you choose to play music and find yourself singing or thinking about the song rather than focusing on God. . . it is time to turn off the music. However, if you play music with words, it is entirely possible to hear a song that draws you closer to Christ through the words. Personally, there are many songs that bring tears to my eyes when I sing them. Music is yet another form of worship, so if it touches your heart, go for it. I just caution you not to let your entire prayer time be a song fest. You can always spend "additional" time praising God through music later in the day.

When my wife and I visited the Holy Land, we purchased prayer shawls (Hebrew – tallit). The tallit is worn over your outer clothing during morning prayers. It has twined or knotted fringes attached to its four corners. The Bible does not command wearing a unique shawl or tallit, but presumes that people wore a garment of some kind to cover themselves and instructs them to add fringes to the four corners (Numbers 15.38). My wife and I always wear our shawls on Maundy Thursday prayer vigils at our church.

My Christian mentor, Albatross, gave me a "clinging cross" many years ago. It is a small 4" cross designed and form fitted to the hand to be held by individuals during their prayer time. I hold my cross in my hand every day during prayers. Somehow and for some reason the cross seems to put the hand of Jesus in my hand (Psalm 73.23). It seems to bring His presence to my mind as I speak to Him.

The prayer room at our house is adorned with small flags and banners, crosses of various kinds, stained glass window hangings, Christian photos, a keyboard and guitar, and things of sentimental value we have purchased over the years that have brought us closer to Christ. All of these things touch us in ways that are meaningful to us. I would guess that you, too, have similar things to adorn your prayer room/space.

Of course, if ANYTHING in your prayer room/space becomes a distraction to your primary objective, to talk with God, then it needs to be removed.

Other ideas for use outside your prayer room/space might include watching Christian DVDs while you are exercising, saying the Bearpaw Prayer as you exercise, listening to an audio Bible while traveling or exercising, take your own reading material (Bible or devotionals) to the waiting room of dentist, doctor, etc. Be creative, do whatever "sets your heart on fire" for your love of God.

When you pray, walk it out, sing it out, blast it out from a ram's horn, anoint something with oil, hug a prayer cloth, lay your hands on something – whatever. If your motives are pure, you won't offend God. Let your imagination run wild in the enormous posture of His kingdom. Let them flow for the glory of His name.[177]

Day 86

Sin ☹

Let's start off right from the get go and establish the fact that you and I are sinners. You are human, and sin has been a part of your life since birth and will continue to plague you until your death. You can't run away from it or hide from it – and you certainly can't deny it. NO other human on earth has ever lived without sin. . . only Jesus.

"All have sinned and fall short of the glory of God" (Romans 3.23).

"There is not a righteous man on earth who does what is right and never sins" (Ecclesiastes 7.20).

Hamartiology is the branch of theology that deals with the study of sin. It investigates how sin originated, how it affects the human race, the different types and degrees of sin, and the result of sin. As you might guess, you could spend hours, days, months, even years delving into the study of sin.

Most likely you have the general ideas about sin, so we will discuss only the basic topics relevant to sin in your life and how it affects prayer.

This small three letter word has monumental impact on your prayer life. You know that sin is the breaking of God's law and His will for you. If God says "do not lie" and you lie, then you have broken His law and sinned. And so, when you sin you have offended God because His law is moral purity and perfect. You have in essence separated yourself from God. And thus, by separating yourself from God by breaking His law you have placed yourself in God's judgment. "Your sins have made a separation between you and your God" (Isaiah 59.2) and "The wages of sin is death" (Romans 6.23).

Of course, you know there is good news ahead. Jesus came to take our place and die for our sins. "He himself bore our sins in His body on the tree, so that we might die to sins and live for righteousness; by his wounds you have been healed" (1 Peter 2.24). This means that anyone who trusts and believes what Jesus did on the cross will have his sins removed.

Is your sin a repeated behavior? If so, this can be especially frustrating. If you have a heart for God, you have probably confessed it a thousand times, only to fall a thousand more times. What can break you out of this cycle? There are several answers: the Holy Spirit, the Word of God, and the fellowship and accountability of other believers are all elements of your growth in Christlikeness. But there is a root to your problem that perhaps you haven't acknowledged and confessed. The real problem – the first sin that led to your behavior – is that you possibly were not in awe of God enough to stop and think about your actions. You forgot that you were on holy ground – and in holy company. You forgot that God is always with you and even in you.[178]

God searches minds and hearts. Nothing is hidden from God – this can be either terrifying or comforting. Your thoughts are an open book to Him. Because God knows even your motives, you have no place to hide, no way to pretend you can get away with sin. But that very knowledge also gives you great comfort. You don't have to impress God or put up a false front. Instead, you can trust God to help you work through your weaknesses in order to serve Him as He planned.[179]

 In The Name Of Jesus by Susie McEntire

Day 87

Don't Be a Quitter

Y ou are approaching Day 90 and the end of this book. I truly hope you have been faithful in your commitment of prayer to God. And I hope this book has enlightened you about prayer and created a "monster of a prayer warrior" within you.

It will soon be solely your responsibility to pray each day. I feel confident you have good intentions of doing this, but I also know of the great lies, temptations, and false ideas Satan will place before you. Trust me, he will do everything in his sneaky power to get you to stop praying.

Through your reading and study of the Bible, you know that all twelve of Jesus' original disciples bailed on Him. At one point they all deserted Him. "Then everyone deserted him and fled" (Mark 14.50). They fled like a covey of frightened quail. And of course, Peter – the rock, the one Christ would build His church upon – went on to deny Christ three more times. "Before the rooster crows today, you will disown me three times" (Luke 22.61).

I know your intentions right now are good. I know you "plan" on praying every day. And. . . I know you, too, will bail on Christ. You will not be by yourself, we have all done it. We are all guilty. We have all left Him "hanging."

But your Savior wants only the best for you. He wants you to spend eternity with Him. So He will never give up on you. "Never will I leave you, never will I forsake you" (Hebrews 13.5). Just as He forgave His disciples when they left Him in His most urgent time of need, He will also forgive you in your failure to be as faithful as you wish to be.

When you feel like giving up, when you feel like quitting, turn to Scripture for reassurance.

"Be strong and courageous. Do not be afraid or terrified because of them, for the Lord your God goes with you; He will never leave you nor forsake you" (Deuteronomy 31.6).

"Have I not commanded you? Be strong and courageous. Do not be terrified; do not be discouraged, for the Lord your God will be with you wherever you go" (Joshua 1.9).

"It is God who arms me with strength and makes my way perfect" (Psalm 18.32).

"The Lord is my strength and my shield; my heart trusts in him and I am helped" (Psalm 28.7).

"But those who hope in the Lord will renew their strength. They will soar on wings like eagles, they will run and not grow weary, they will walk and not be faint" (Isaiah 40.31).

"Do you not know that in a race all the runners run, but only one gets the prize? Run in such a way as to get the prize" (1 Corinthians 9.24).

"Be strong in the Lord and in His mighty power" (Ephesians 6.10).

Do you have a verse that you turn to for strength?

_____
_____
_____
_____

Day 88

Reflection

Often in our prayers we ask to be formed more into the image of Jesus. After all, He was the only perfect human being to walk the face of the earth. Who wouldn't want to be like Him? I am convinced that as you spend more time in prayer with Him and spend more time in study of Him you become more like Him, and that is a great thing!

The Great Commission (Matthew 28.16-20) says in black and white (and red) that you are to go out and make disciples of all nations. You are to go out into our world and tell others about your Savior, Jesus Christ. To some that may be a bit scary because it sounds a lot like *evangelism*. I can see the fear in your eyes. I can read your thoughts from right here in Colorado. . . "Whoa pal, I signed up to learn more about prayer, not to become a traveling preacher – a 21st century John the Baptist." My words to you are. . . . "RELAX, you are already making an impression on others."

You see, each of us (yourself included) is some sort of reflection to those with whom we come in contact. You are affecting people even when you are not trying to. The question of most importance is just what are you reflecting to those people? I think most people would say they want to make a positive impression and thus a positive impact on others.

In time, people—your friends and those close to you—are going to notice a change in you. They are going to notice a different and possibly new side of you. Your time with God is absolutely going to change you. Some may comment about this change to you, while others may not. Some may indeed be specific about your attitude and personality changing. . . but just can't put their finger on what has motivated this change.

"May others see You, Lord, in me." Do you include this in your prayers? I personally pray for this every day. Do others see the radiance of Christ glowing from within you? Do others see a humble, helping characteristic in you or do you reflect a haughty, highly-visible personality? Do others see a person filled with love, patience, understanding, compassion, forgiveness, kindness, joy, and peace – or do they see a person that is a hypocrite, arrogant, and self-centered? Do they see Jesus or do they see a Pharisee? Read this carefully, "We all reflect some sort of image to others." Because of the free will you have been given, you have the choice as to what you reflect.

King David said, "Those who look to Him are radiant" (Psalm 34.5). **KING** David said that. Did you notice that, the **KING** of Israel said to look to and reflect "God", not to reflect himself, the king. Look up to God; let His radiance fill your face with a smile of love and confidence. You are His child; let others see that in you.

"And we, who with unveiled faces all reflect the Lord's glory, are being transformed into his likeness with ever-increasing glory, which comes from the Lord, who is the Spirit" (2 Corinthians 3.18). You were made in the image of God (Genesis 1.26) and you were made to reflect His glory. You do not have to preach from a pulpit for "you are a chosen people, a royal priesthood" (1 Peter 2.9). You "preach" to others by every action and every word you say. So, what are you preaching?

Lord, may Your loving light shine through my life to light the way for others, and may others see You, Lord, in me.

Day 89

Bearpaw Samples

Closing Prayers

When you have finished your conversation with God, I think it is best to offer some closing thoughts and prayers instead of just getting up and leaving the room. I have listed some of the prayers I close with each day ONLY as examples and ideas of what you may choose to do. As your time with God develops, you will no doubt have prayers and Scripture that is especially meaningful to you.

Before beginning my closing prayers, I spend some time in silence and listen for God's word.

"Lord, I come to you today seeking to hear Your voice. All too often I do all the talking, failing to allow You to share Your Word, wisdom, and will for me. Give me the courage to quietly listen as Your loving presence surrounds me. May I be drawn ever closer to You through Your words and through Your love.

Then I begin concluding my conversation with God.

"Father, I am wholly yours today. Use me as you see fit."[180]
"Lord Jesus Christ, Son of God, have mercy on me, a sinner" (Jesus prayer).
"Not my will, but yours be done" (Luke 22.42).
"Create in me a clean heart, O God, and renew a right spirit within me" (Psalm 51.10 NLT).
"Whatever you do, do it all for the glory of God" (1 Corinthians 10.31).
"Love the Lord your God with all your heart and with all your soul and with all your strength and with all your mind; and love your neighbor as yourself" (Luke 10.27).
"I can do all things through Christ who gives me strength" (Philippians 4.3 NKJV).
"Sing praises to the glory of God's name" (Psalm 66.2 CEB).
"May your loving light shine through my life to light the way for others."
"May others see You, Lord, in me."
"Father God, thank you for Your love and Your presence with me, today and always" (Bearpaw Prayer).

Upon completion of my closing prayers, I stand before a photo of Jesus and thank Him for being present with me.

 Revelation Song by Newsboys

Day __90__

The End

My friend, we have reached the end of this journey together. But know this, you will NEVER be alone. "I am with you always" (Matthew 28.20). From this point on you will travel with God. Trust me, you are in much better hands.

You will never master the skill of prayer; it is an activity of progressive learning. Don't be afraid to try different approaches to your prayer style and format; change is good.

Nothing is carved in stone. . . (well, the Ten Commandments), Nothing is permanent. . . (well, God's unending love). Otherwise, be willing to change, modify, and grow.

Continue to ask God in leading you to more effective prayer. Ask Him to bring you closer to Him and more like Jesus.

As time progresses on and you feel more comfortable and experienced, I hope you will also increase the amount of time you spend in prayer.

I suspect that some readers of this book will have given up before reaching this page. Sadly, some will realize they did not want to pray as much as they thought they did. Some, honestly, just didn't want to make the commitment and give the time needed to God. But you. . .you kept your promise! I thank you, but God is especially happy to be developing this relationship with you.

I encourage you to complete this 90 day journey again in six months or a year. See if your needs are the same or if something new is placed on your heart. As your time with God increases you will hopefully modify your habits of prayer into your own style.

What would you do if your life **depended** on prayer?

If this were your last day on earth, Who or what would you pray for?

So, <u>KNOW</u> this:

I include you and any others that may read this book in MY daily personal prayers. If you recall Day 32, you know I mean that. I truly desire for you to come closer to Christ and His unending love, and I know that can happen through prayer.

God's grace, peace, and blessings be with you as you pray.

Luke 10.27

 Beautiful Things by Gungor

Bible Verses

Scripture used in this book

"The Lord does not look at the things man looks at. Man looks at the outward appearance, but the Lord looks at the heart" (1 Samuel 16.7).

"I will remove from them their heart of stone" (Ezekiel 11.19).

"Search me, O God, and know my heart" (Psalm 139.23).

"Devote yourself to prayer" (Colossians 4.2).

"Blessed is the one who reads the words of this prophecy, and blessed are those who hear it and take to heart what is written in it" (Revelation 1.3).

"Apply your heart to what I teach" (Proverbs 22.17).

"Neither death nor life, neither angels nor demons, neither the present nor the future, nor any powers, neither height nor depth, nor anything else in all creation, will be able to separate us from the love of God that is in Christ Jesus our Lord" (Romans 8.38-39).

"For God so loved the world that he gave his one and only Son, that whoever believes in him shall not perish but have eternal life." (John 3.16)

"Love the Lord your God with all your heart and with all your soul and with all your strength and with all your mind, and, Love your neighbor as yourself" (Luke 10.27).

"The prayer of a righteous man is powerful and effective" (James 5.16).

"In bitterness of soul Hannah wept much and prayed to the Lord. And she made a vow saying, 'O Lord Almighty, if you will only look upon your servant's misery and remember me, and not forget your servant but give her a son, then I will give him to the Lord for all the days of his life, and no razor will ever be used on his head'" (1 Samuel 1.10-11).

"There was also a prophetess, Anna, the daughter of Phanuel, of the tribe of Asher. She was very old; she had lived with her husband seven years after her marriage, and then was a widow until she was eighty-four. She never left the temple but worshiped night and day, fasting and praying. She gave thanks to God and spoke about the child to all who were looking forward to the redemption of Jerusalem" (Luke 2.36-38).

"Be strong and courageous" (Deuteronomy 31.6).

"In the morning, O Lord, you hear my voice; in the morning I lay my requests before you and wait in expectation" (Psalm 5.3).

"But I cry to you for help, O Lord; in the morning my prayer comes before you" (Psalm 88.13).

"Now Moses used to take a tent and pitch it outside the camp some distance away, calling it the 'tent of meeting'" (Exodus 33.17).

"When you pray, go into your room, close the door and pray to your Father, who is unseen" (Matthew 6.6).

"For everyone who exalts himself will be humbled, and he who humbles himself will be exalted" (Luke 18.14).

"For your Father knows what you need before you ask Him" (Matthew 6.8).

"Do not be like the hypocrites" (Matthew 6.5).

"O Lord, you have searched me and you know me" (Psalm 139.1).

"As a young man marries a maiden, so will your sons marry you; as a bridegroom rejoices over his bride, so will your God rejoice over you" (Isaiah 62.5).

"I am with you and will watch over you wherever you go" (Genesis 28.15).

"When you ask, you do not receive, because you ask with wrong motives, that you may spend what you get on your pleasures" (James 4.3).

"Not my will, but yours be done" (Luke 22.42).

"I am the Lord's servant," Mary answered. "Let it be to me as you have said" (Luke 1.38).

"If you remain in me and my words remain in you, ask whatever you wish, and it will be given you" (John 15.7).

"Many are the plans in a man's heart, but it is the Lord's purpose that prevails" (Proverbs 19.21).

"For my Father's will is that everyone who looks to the Son and believes in him shall have eternal life" (John 6.40).

"It is God's will that you should be sanctified" (1 Thessalonians 4.3).

"Be joyful always; pray continually; give thanks in all circumstances, for this is God's will for you in Christ Jesus" (1 Thessalonians 5.16-18).

"For it is God's will that by doing good you should silence the ignorant talk of foolish men" (1 Peter 2.15).

"There is neither Jew nor Greek, slave nor free, male nor female, for you are all one in Christ Jesus" (Galatians 3.28).

"Ask and it will be given to you" (Matthew 7.7).

"Far be it from me that I should sin against the Lord by failing to pray for you" (1 Samuel 12.23).

"Therefore he (Jesus) is able to save completely those who come to God through him, because he always lives to intercede for them" (Hebrews 7.25).

"We do not know what we ought to pray for, but the Spirit himself intercedes for us" (Romans 8.26).

"I urge then, first of all, that requests, prayers, intercession and thanksgiving be made for everyone" (1 Timothy 2.1).

"Love the Lord you God with all your heart and with all your soul and with all your mind. This is the first and greatest commandment. And the second is like it: 'Love your neighbor as yourself.' All the law and the prophets hang on these two commandments" (Matthew 22.37-40).

"If I had cherished sin in my heart, the Lord would not have listened" (Psalm 66.18).

"If we confess our sins, he is faithful and just and will forgive us our sins and purify us from all unrighteousness: (1 John 1.9).

"O you of little faith" (Matthew 6.30).

"If you believe, you will receive whatever you ask for in prayer" (Matthew 21.22).

"There are different kinds of working, but the same God works all of them in all men" (1 Corinthians 12.6).

"There is no one who does good, not even one" (Psalm 14.3).

"There is no one righteous, not even one" (Romans 3.10).

"There is not a righteous man on earth who does what is right and never sins" (Ecclesiastes 7.20).

"If we confess our sins, he is faithful and just and will forgive us our sins and purify us from all unrighteousness" (1John 1.9).

"For I will forgive their wickedness and will remember their sins no more" (Hebrews 8.12).

"Nothing in all creation is hidden from God" (Hebrews 4.13).

"For a man's ways are in full view of the Lord" (Proverbs 5.21).

"Create in me a clean heart, O God, and renew a right spirit within me" (Psalm 51.10).

"For if you forgive men when they sin against you, your heavenly Father will also forgive you. But if you do not forgive men their sins, your Father will not forgive your sins" (Matthew 6.14-15).

"Bear with each other and forgive whatever grievances you may have against one another. Forgive as the Lord forgave you" (Colossians 3.13).

"Father, forgive them, for they do not know what they are doing" (Luke 23.34).

"Be on your guard against the yeast of the Pharisees, which is hypocrisy" (Luke 12.1).

"Two men went up to the temple to pray, one a Pharisee and the other a tax collector. The Pharisee stood up and prayed about himself: 'God, I thank you that I am not like other men – robbers, evildoers, adulterers, - or even like this tax collector. I fast twice a week and give a tenth of all I get.' But the tax collector stood at a distance. He would not even look up to heaven, but beat his breast and said, 'God, have mercy on me, a sinner.' I tell you that this man, rather than the other, went home justified before God. For everyone who exalts himself will be humbled, and he who humbles himself will be exalted" (Luke 18.9-14).

"Apply your heart to what I teach" (Proverbs 22.17).

"Pray continually" (1 Thessalonians 5.17).

"Devote yourself to prayer, being watchful and thankful" (Colossians 4.2).

"I will not leave you" (Genesis 28.15).

"Hear, O Israel: The Lord our God, the Lord is one. Love the Lord your God with all your heart and with all your soul and with all your strength. These commandments that I give you today are to be upon your hearts. Impress them on your children. Talk about them when you sit at home and when you walk along the road, when you lie down and when you get up. Tie them as symbols on your hands and bind them on your foreheads. Write them on the door-frames of your houses and on your gates" (Deuteronomy 6.4-9).

"Oh, that you would bless me and enlarge my territory! Let your hand be with me, and keep me from harm so that I will be free from pain" (1 Chronicles 4.10). "And God granted his request" (1 Chronicles 4.10).

"If you believe, you will believe whatever you ask for in prayer" (Matthew 21.22).

"I will praise you, O Lord, with all my heart" (Psalm 9.1).

"Sing and make music in your heart to the Lord" (Ephesians 5.19).

"We also thank God continually" (1 Thessalonians 2.13).

"I constantly remember you in my prayers" (2 Timothy 1.3).

"Jesus, Son of David, have mercy on me!" (Luke 18.38).

"Jesus, Master, have pity on us!" (Luke 17.13).

"God, have mercy on me a sinner" (Luke 18.13).

"When you pray, do not keep on babbling like pagans, for they think they will be heard because of their many words" (Matthew 6.7).

"Could you not keep watch for one hour" (Matthew 14.37)?

"Watch and pray" (Matthew 14.38).

"Well done, good and faithful servant!" (Matthew 25.21).

"Faith comes from hearing the message, and the message is heard through the Word of Christ" (Romans 10.17).

"If you believe, you will receive whatever you ask for in prayer" (Matthew 21.22).

"Some men brought to him a paralytic, lying on a mat. When Jesus saw their faith,. . . (he healed the man)" (Matthew 9.2).

"Immediately Jesus reached out his hand and caught him (Peter). 'You of little faith,' he said, 'why did you doubt'" (Matthew 14.31)?

"I tell you the truth, if you have faith as small as a mustard seed, you can say to this mountain, 'move from here to there' and it will move. Nothing will be impossible for you" (Matthew 17.20).

"I tell you the truth, if you have faith and do not doubt. . . ." (Matthew 21.21).

"I am with you always" (Matthew 28.20).

"I am with you and will watch over you wherever you go" (Genesis 28.15).

"Never will I leave you, never will I forsake you" (Hebrews 13.5).

"God will be with you wherever you go" (Joshua 1.9).

"I have made you and I will carry you" (Isaiah 46.4).

"When you fast, do not look somber as the hypocrites do, for they disfigure their faces to show men they are fasting. I tell you the truth, they have received their reward in full. But when you fast, put oil on your head and wash your face, so that it will not be obvious to men that you are fasting, but only to your Father, who is in unseen; and your Father, who sees what is done in secret, will reward you" (Matthew 6.16-18).

"In the beginning was the Word, and the Word was with God, and the Word was God" (John 1.1).

"All Scripture is God-breathed and is useful for teaching, rebuking, correcting and training in righteousness" (2 Timothy 3.16).

"Here I am! I stand at the door and knock. If anyone hears my voice and opens the door, I will come in and eat with him, and he with me" (Revelation 3.20).

"He is with you and will watch over you wherever you go" (Genesis 28.15).

"Teach me your way, O Lord, and I will walk in your truth" (Psalm 86.11).

"I will instruct and teach you in the way you should go" (Psalm 32.8).

"Man does not live by bread alone, but on every word that comes from the mouth of God" (Matthew 4.4).

"Reflect on what I am saying, for the Lord will give you insight into all this" (2 Timothy 2.7).

"For the Lord your God will be with you wherever you go" (Joshua 1.9).

"Then you will know the truth, and the truth shall set you free" (John 8.32)

"I call on you, O God, for you will answer me" (Psalm 17.6).

"Ask and it shall be given to you. . ." (Matthew 7.7).

"For where two or three come together in my name, there I am with them" (Matthew 18.20)

"If you believe, you will receive whatever you ask for in prayer" (Matthew 21.22).

"You may ask me for anything in my name, and I will do it" (John 14.14).

"If we ask anything according to his will, he hears us" (1 John 5.14).

"Whatever you ask for in prayer, believe that you have received it, and it will be yours" (Mark 11.24).

"My Father will give you whatever you ask in my name" (John 16.23).

"For this reason, since the day we heard about you, we have not stopped praying for you and asking God to fill you with the knowledge of his will through all spiritual wisdom and understanding. And we pray this in order that you may live a life worthy of the Lord and may please him in every way; bearing fruit in every good work, growing in the knowledge of God, being strengthened with all power according to his glorious might so that you may have great endurance and patience, and joyfully giving thanks to the Father, who has qualified you to share in the inheritance of the saints in the kingdom of light" (Colossians 1.9-12).

"Come, O Lord" (1 Corinthians 16.22).

"You may ask for anything in my name, and I will do it" (John 14.14)

"If any of you lacks wisdom, he should ask God, who gives generously to all without finding fault, and it will be given to him" (James 1.5).

"Together with all those everywhere who call on the name of our Lord Jesus Christ" (1 Corinthians 1.2).

"Sing and make music in your heart to the Lord" (Ephesians 5.19).

"Repent of this wickedness and pray to the Lord" (Acts 8.22).

"My Lord and my God" (John 20.28).

"My Father will give you whatever you ask in my name" (John 16.23).

"Then they prayed, Lord you know everyone's heart" (Acts 1.24).

"I am going to send you what my Father has promised; but stay in the city until you have been clothed with power from on high" (Luke 24.49).

"Receive the Holy Spirit" (John 20.22).

"In the same way, the Spirit helps us in our weakness. We do not know what we ought to pray for, but the Spirit himself intercedes for us with groans that words cannot express" (Romans 8.26).

"But you dear friends, build yourselves up in your most holy faith and pray in the Holy Spirit" (Jude 20).

"Come, follow me" (Matthew 4.19).

"If anyone comes to me and does not hate his father and mother, his wife and children, his brothers and sisters – yes, even his own life – he cannot be my disciple. And anyone who does not carry his cross and follow me cannot be my disciple" (Luke 14.25-27).

"If you confess with your mouth, 'Jesus is Lord,' and believe in your heart that God raised him from the dead, you will be saved. For it is with your heart that you believe and are justified, and it is with your mouth that you confess and are saved" (Romans 10.9-10).

"All authority in heaven and on earth has been given to me. Therefore go and make disciples of all nations, baptizing them in the name of the Father and of the Son and of the Holy Spirit, and teaching them to obey everything I have commanded you. And surely, I am with you always, to the very end of the age" (Matthew 28.18-20).

"Be joyful always, pray continually, give thanks in all circumstances, for this is God's will for you in Christ Jesus" (1 Thessalonians 5.16-18).

"All have sinned and fall short of the glory of God" (Romans 3.23).

"There is not a righteous man on earth who does what is right and never sins" (Ecclesiastes 7.20).

"Your sins have made a separation between you and your God" (Isaiah 59.2).

"The wages of sin is death" (Romans 6.23).

"He himself bore our sins in his body on the tree, so that we might die to sins and live for righteousness; by his wounds you have been healed" (1 Peter 2.24).

"Then everyone deserted him and fled" (Mark 14.50).

"Before the rooster crows today, you will disown me three times" (Luke 22.61).

"Never will I leave you, never will I forsake you" (Hebrews 13.5).

"Be strong and courageous. Do not be afraid or terrified because of them, for the Lord your God goes with you; he will never leave you nor forsake you" (Deuteronomy 31.6).

"Have I not commanded you? Be strong and courageous. Do not be terrified; do not be discouraged, for the Lord your God will be with you wherever you go" (Joshua 1.9).

"It is God who arms me with strength and makes my way perfect" (Psalm 18.32).

"The Lord is my strength and my shield; my heart trusts in him and I am helped" (Psalm 28.7).

"But those who hope in the Lord will renew their strength. They will soar on wings like eagles, they will run and not grow weary, they will walk and not be faint" (Isaiah 40.31).

"Do you not know that in a race all the runners run, but only one gets the prize? Run in such a way as to get the prize" (1 Corinthians 9.24).

"Be strong in the Lord and in his mighty power" (Ephesians 6.10).

"And we, who with unveiled faces all reflect the Lord's glory, are being transformed into his likeness with ever-increasing glory, which comes from the Lord, who is the Spirit" (2 Corinthians 3.18).

"You are a chosen people, a royal priesthood" (1 Peter 2.9).

"Not my will, but yours be done" (Luke 22.42).

"Create in me a clean heart, Oh God, and renew a right spirit within me" (Psalm 51.10 NLT).

"Whatever you do, do it all for the glory of God" (1 Corinthians 10.31).

"Love the Lord your God with all your heart and with all your soul and with all your strength and with all your mind; and love your neighbor as yourself" (Luke 10.27).

"I can do all things through Christ who gives me strength" (Philippians 4.3 NKJV).

"Sing praises to the glory of God's name" (Psalm 66.2 CEB).

"I am with you always" (Matthew 28.20).

Music Bearpaw Has Suggested

Draw Me Close To You
In His Time
Unfailing Love
Friend of God
He Knows My Name
God Will Make a Way
Everything Cries Holy
Can I Pray For You
At the Foot of the Cross
Grace Flows Down
What a Friend We Have In Jesus
The Lord's Prayer
Make Me a Channel of Your Peace
As We Worship You
I Will Sing
Open the Eyes of My Heart
Blessings
Footprints in the Sand
Thy Word
10,000 Reasons
In the Name of Jesus
Revelation Song
Beautiful Things

End Notes

1   Cymbala, Jim. Breakthrough Prayer. Grand Rapids. Zondervan. 2003. Pg 33

2   Foster, Richard J. Prayer: Finding The Heart's True Home. New York. HarperCollins Publishers. 1992. Pg 8

3   Munroe, Myles. Understanding The Purpose And Power Of Prayer. New Kensington. Whitaker House. 2002. Pg 109

4   Bounds, E. M. The Power Of Prayer. Christian Art Gifts. 2007. June 14

5   Yancey, Philip. Prayer: Does It Make Any Difference. Grand Rapids. Zondervan. 2006. Pg 35

6   Meyer, Joyce. The Power Of Simple Prayer; How To Talk To God About Everything. New York. Faith Words. 2007. Pg 10

7   Meyer, Joyce. The Power Of Simple Prayer; How To Talk To God About Everything. New York. Faith Words. 2007. Pg viii

8   Our Daily Bread Daily Devotional. Grand Rapids. RBC Ministries. 12.19.2012

9   Bernard, Daniel. Praying Up A Storm. Shippensburg. Treasure House. 2004. Pg25

10   Henry, Matthew. Matthew Henry's Commentary On The Whole Bible. Peabody. Hendrickson Publishers, Inc. 1991. Vol 2. Pg 378

11   Meyer, Joyce. The Power Of Simple Prayer; How To Talk To God About Everything. New York. Faith Words. 2007. Pg 14

12   Rosscup, Jim. Exposition On Prayer: Igniting The Flame To Fuel Our Communication With God. Chattanooga. AMG Publishers. 2011. New Testament Volume 1. Pg 1419

13   Arthur, Kay. Lord, Teach Me To Pray In 28 Days. Eugene. Harvest House Publishers. 2008. Pg 44

14 Galli, Mark & Bell, James S. The Complete Idiots Guide To Prayer. New York. Alpha Books. 2004. Pg 212

15 Foster, Richard J. Prayer: Finding The Heart's True Home. New York. HarperCollins Publishers. 1992. Pg 1

16 Stanley, Charles F. In Touch. Atlanta. In Touch Ministries. 2013. 4-15-13. Pg 50

17 Alves, Elizabeth. Becoming A Prayer Warrior. Ventura. Regal Books. 1998. Pg22

18 Arthur, Kay. Lord, Teach Me To Pray In 28 Days. Eugene. Harvest House Publishers. 2008. Pg 33

19 Yancey, Philip. Prayer: Does It Make Any Difference. Grand Rapids. Zondervan. 2006. Pg 56

20 Cymbala, Jim. Breakthrough Prayer. Grand Rapids. Zondervan. 2003. Pg 143

21 Rosscup, Jim. Exposition On Prayer: Igniting The Flame To Fuel Our Communication With God. Chattanooga. AMG Publishers. 2011. New Testament Volume 2. Pg 2247

22 Damazio, Frank. Season of Intercession. Portland. City Bible Publishing. 1998. Pg 16

23 Arthur, Kay. Lord, Teach Me To Pray In 28 Days. Eugene. Harvest House Publishers. 2008. Pg 11

24 O'Neill, Robert The Right Reverend. Pastoral Letter To The Diocese Of Colorado. Denver. Bishop of the Episcopal Diocese of Colorado. July 2012.

25 Arthur, Kay. Lord, Teach Me To Pray In 28 Days. Eugene. Harvest House Publishers. 2008. Pg 58

26 Cymbala, Jim. Breakthrough Prayer. Grand Rapids. Zondervan. 2003. Pg 24

27 Arthur, Kay. Lord, Teach Me To Pray In 28 Days. Eugene. Harvest House Publishers. 2008. Pg 43

28 Munroe, Myles. Understanding The Purpose And Power Of Prayer. New Kensington. Whitaker House. 2002. Pg 186

29 Bounds, E.M. The Complete Works Of E.M. Bounds On Prayer. Grand Rapids. Baker Books. 1990. Pg 326

30 Bounds, E. M. The Power Of Prayer. Christian Art Gifts. 2007. May 27

31 Bounds, E. M. The Power Of Prayer. Christian Art Gifts. 2007. September 20

32 Henry, Matthew. Matthew Henry's Commentary On The Whole Bible. Peabody. Hendrickson Publishers, Inc. 1991. Vol 6. Pg 902

33 Young, Sarah. Jesus Calling. Nashville. Thomas Nelson. 2004. Pg 115

34 Meyer, Joyce. The Power Of Simple Prayer; How To Talk To God About Everything. New York. Faith Words. 2007. Pg 23

35 Meyer, Joyce. The Power Of Simple Prayer; How To Talk To God About Everything. New York. Faith Words. 2007. Pg 23

[36] Bounds, E. M. The Power Of Prayer. Christian Art Gifts. 2007. January 20

[37] Bounds, E.M. The Complete Works Of E.M. Bounds On Prayer. Grand Rapids. Baker Books. 1990. Pg 82

[38] Bounds, E.M. The Complete Works Of E.M. Bounds On Prayer. Grand Rapids. Baker Books. 1990. Pg 57

[39] Yancey, Philip. Prayer: Does It Make Any Difference. Grand Rapids. Zondervan. 2006. Pg 60

[40] Bringman, Randy. Canon City, CO. 81212

[41] Tiegreen, Chris. One Year Devotional: Worship The King. Carol Stream. Tyndale House Publishers, Inc. 2008. March 1

[42] Our Daily Bread Daily Devotional. Grand Rapids. RBC Ministries. 2.14.2013

[43] Murrow, David. Why Men Hate Going To Church. Nashville. Thomas Nelson, Inc. 2005. Pg 28

[44] Bounds, E.M. The Complete Works Of E.M. Bounds On Prayer. Grand Rapids. Baker Books. 1990. Pg 82

[45] Bounds, E.M. The Complete Works Of E.M. Bounds On Prayer. Grand Rapids. Baker Books. 1990. Pg 113

[46] Bounds, E.M. The Complete Works Of E.M. Bounds On Prayer. Grand Rapids. Baker Books. 1990. Pg 331

[47] Tiegreen, Chris. Creative Prayer. Colorado Springs. Multnomah Books. 2007. Pg 38

[48] Rosscup, Jim. Exposition On Prayer: Igniting The Flame To Fuel Our Communication With God. Chattanooga. AMG Publishers. 2011. Old Testament Volume 1. Pg 345

[49] The Church Pension Fund. Prayer Book And Hymnal Containing The Book Of Common Prayer And The Hymnal 1982: According To The Use Of The Episcopal Church. New York. Church Publishing Incorporated. 1986. Proper 22. Pg 234

[50] Exley, Patterson, Hummel, Edwards. Daybreak With God. Tulsa. Honor Books. 1999. Pg 39

[51] Foster, Richard J. Prayer: Finding The Heart's True Home. New York. HarperCollins Publishers. 1992. Pg 74

[52] NIV Archeological Study Bible. Grand Rapids. The Zondervan Corporation. 2005. Bible Footnotes. Pg 1771

[53] Bounds, E.M. The Complete Works Of E.M. Bounds On Prayer. Grand Rapids. Baker Books. 1990. Pg 464

[54] Henry, Matthew. Matthew Henry's Commentary On The Whole Bible. Peabody. Hendrickson Publishers, Inc. 1991. Vol 3. Pg 207

[55] Life Application Study Bible. THE HOLY BIBLE, NEW INTERNATIONAL VERSION ®. Carol Stream. Tyndale House Publishers, Inc. 2005. Pg 828

56 Bounds, E.M. The Complete Works Of E.M. Bounds On Prayer. Grand Rapids. Baker Books. 1990. Pg 301

57 Bounds, E.M. The Complete Works Of E.M. Bounds On Prayer. Grand Rapids. Baker Books. 1990. Pg 343

58 Forward Day By Day Daily Devotional. Cincinnati. Forward Movement. 3.27.2013

59 Bounds, E.M. The Complete Works Of E.M. Bounds On Prayer. Grand Rapids. Baker Books. 1990. Pg 86

60 Bounds, E.M. The Complete Works Of E.M. Bounds On Prayer. Grand Rapids. Baker Books. 1990. Pg 88

61 Bounds, E. M. The Power Of Prayer. Christian Art Gifts. 2007. February 23

62 Tiegreen, Chris. One Year Devotional: Worship The King. Carol Stream. Tyndale House Publishers, Inc. 2008. March 27. Pg 86

63 Life Application Study Bible. THE HOLY BIBLE, NEW INTERNATIONAL VERSION ®. Carol Stream. Tyndale House Publishers, Inc. 2005. Pg 831

64 Rafael Cardinal Merry del Val. 1865-1930. Secretary of State for Pope Saint Pius X

65 Damazio,Frank. Season of Intercession. Portland. City Bible Publishing. 1998. Pg 181

66 Bounds, E. M. The Power Of Prayer. Christian Art Gifts. 2007. October 13

67

68 Bounds, E. M. The Power Of Prayer. Christian Art Gifts. 2007. April 17

69 Young, Sarah. Jesus Calling. Nashville. Thomas Nelson. 2004. Pg 24

70 Galli, Mark & Bell, James S. The Complete Idiots Guide To Prayer. New York. Alpha Books. 2004. Pg 5

71 Foster, Richard J. Prayer: Finding The Heart's True Home. New York. HarperCollins Publishers. 1992. Pg 9

72 Meyer, Joyce. The Power Of Simple Prayer; How To Talk To God About Everything. New York. Faith Words. 2007. Pg 6

73 Galli, Mark & Bell, James S. The Complete Idiots Guide To Prayer. New York. Alpha Books. 2004. Pg 8

74 Damazio,Frank. Season of Intercession. Portland. City Bible Publishing. 1998. Pg 77

75 Cymbala, Jim. Breakthrough Prayer. Grand Rapids. Zondervan. 2003. Pg 148

76 Munroe, Myles. Understanding The Purpose And Power Of Prayer. New Kensington. Whitaker House. 2002. Pg 22

77 Young, William P. The Shack. Newbury Park. Windblown Media. 2007. Pg 92

[78] Munroe, Myles. Understanding The Purpose And Power Of Prayer. New Kensington. Whitaker House. 2002. Pg 2

[79] Young, Sarah. Jesus Calling. Nashville. Thomas Nelson. 2004. Pg 48

[80] Stanway, Alfred. Prayer: A Personal Testimony. Melbourne. Acorn Press Ltd. 2000. Pg 22

[81] Young, Sarah. Jesus Calling. Nashville. Thomas Nelson. 2004. Pg 13

[82] Henry, Matthew. Matthew Henry's Commentary On The Whole Bible. Peabody. Hendrickson Publishers, Inc. 1991. Vol 6. Pg 796

[83] Munroe, Myles. Understanding The Purpose And Power Of Prayer. New Kensington. Whitaker House. 2002. Pg 39

[84] Munroe, Myles. Understanding The Purpose And Power Of Prayer. New Kensington. Whitaker House. 2002. Pg 40

[85] Munroe, Myles. Understanding The Purpose And Power Of Prayer. New Kensington. Whitaker House. 2002. Pg 191

[86] Munroe, Myles. Understanding The Purpose And Power Of Prayer. New Kensington. Whitaker House. 2002. Pg 44

[87] Cymbala, Jim. Breakthrough Prayer. Grand Rapids. Zondervan. 2003. Pg 92

[88] Young, Sarah. Jesus Calling. Nashville. Thomas Nelson. 2004. Pg 6

[89] Bounds, E.M. The Complete Works Of E.M. Bounds On Prayer. Grand Rapids. Baker Books. 1990. Pg 70

[90] Life Application Study Bible. THE HOLY BIBLE, NEW INTERNATIONAL VERSION ®. Carol Stream. Tyndale House Publishers, Inc. 2005. Pg 832

[91] Blackaby, Henry and Norman. Experiencing Prayer With Jesus. Sisters. Multnomah Publishers. 2006. Pg 81

[92] Arthur, Kay. Lord, Teach Me To Pray In 28 Days. Eugene. Harvest House Publishers. 2008. Pg 115

[93] Meyer, Joyce. The Power Of Simple Prayer; How To Talk To God About Everything. New York. Faith Words. 2007. Pg 9

[94] Foster, Richard J. Prayer: Finding The Heart's True Home. New York. HarperCollins Publishers. 1992. Pg 197

[95] Foster, Richard J. Prayer: Finding The Heart's True Home. New York. HarperCollins Publishers. 1992. Pg 180

[96] Damazio,Frank. Season of Intercession. Portland. City Bible Publishing. 1998. Pg 81

[97] Life Application Study Bible. THE HOLY BIBLE, NEW INTERNATIONAL VERSION ®. Carol Stream. Tyndale House Publishers, Inc. 2005. Pg 2009

[98] Stanway, Alfred. Prayer: A Personal Testimony. Melbourne. Acorn Press Ltd. 2000. Pg 60

[99] Bounds, E. M. The Power Of Prayer. Christian Art Gifts. 2007. February 6

100 Bounds, E. M. The Power Of Prayer. Christian Art Gifts. 2007. July 20

101 Hybels, Bill. Too Busy Not To Pray; Slowing Down To Be With God. Downers Grove. InterVarsity Press. 1998. Pg 65

102 Hybels, Bill. Too Busy Not To Pray; Slowing Down To Be With God. Downers Grove. InterVarsity Press. 1998. Pg 69

103 Hybels, Bill. Too Busy Not To Pray; Slowing Down To Be With God. Downers Grove. InterVarsity Press. 1998. Pg 70

104 Munroe, Myles. Understanding The Purpose And Power Of Prayer. New Kensington. Whitaker House. 2002. Pg 168

105 Cymbala, Jim. Breakthrough Prayer. Grand Rapids. Zondervan. 2003. Pg 52

106 The Church Pension Fund. Prayer Book And Hymnal Containing The Book Of Common Prayer And The Hymnal 1982: According To The Use Of The Episcopal Church. New York. Church Publishing Incorporated. 1986. Proper 22. Pg 360

107 Munroe, Myles. Understanding The Purpose And Power Of Prayer. New Kensington. Whitaker House. 2002. Pg 122

108 Foster, Richard J. Prayer: Finding The Heart's True Home. New York. HarperCollins Publishers. 1992. Pg 187

109 Arthur, Kay. Lord, Teach Me To Pray In 28 Days. Eugene. Harvest House Publishers. 2008. Pg 154

110 Arthur, Kay. Lord, Teach Me To Pray In 28 Days. Eugene. Harvest House Publishers. 2008. Pg 155

111 Kendall, R.T. Total Forgiveness. Lake Mary. Charisma House. 2007. Pg 45

112 Rosscup, Jim. Exposition On Prayer: Igniting The Flame To Fuel Our Communication With God. Chattanooga. AMG Publishers. 2011. Old Testament Volume 1. Pg 556

113 www.Bible.ca/ntx-prayer.htm

114 The Church Pension Fund. Prayer Book And Hymnal Containing The Book Of Common Prayer And The Hymnal 1982: According To The Use Of The Episcopal Church. New York. Church Publishing Incorporated. 1986. Proper 27. Pg 236

115 Stanley, Charles F. In Touch. Atlanta. In Touch Ministries. 2013.

116 Munroe, Myles. Understanding The Purpose And Power Of Prayer. New Kensington. Whitaker House. 2002. Pg 188

117 Stanley, Charles F. In Touch. Atlanta. In Touch Ministries. 2013.

118 Munroe, Myles. Understanding The Purpose And Power Of Prayer. New Kensington. Whitaker House. 2002. Pg 57

119 The Scofield® Study Bible, New American Standard Bible. New York. Oxford University Press, Inc. 2005. Pg 1477

120 Foster, Richard J. Prayer: Finding The Heart's True Home. New York. HarperCollins Publishers. 1992. Pg 7

121 Cymbala, Jim. Breakthrough Prayer. Grand Rapids. Zondervan. 2003. Pg 56

122 www.astrovera.com

123 Wagner, Richard. Christian Prayer For Dummies. New York. Wiley Publishing, Inc. 2003. Pg 99

124 Wagner, Richard. Christian Prayer For Dummies. New York. Wiley Publishing, Inc. 2003. Pg 98

125 Foster, Richard J. Prayer: Finding The Heart's True Home. New York. HarperCollins Publishers. 1992. Pg 155

126 Ward, Thomas R., Jr. Centering Prayer. Cincinnati. Forward Movement Publications. 1997. Pg 12

127 NIV Archeological Study Bible. Grand Rapids. The Zondervan Corporation. 2005. Bible Footnotes. Pg 264

128 Ten Ways To Pray. Cincinnati. Forward Movement Publications. 2010. Pg 3

129 NIV Archeological Study Bible. Grand Rapids. The Zondervan Corporation. 2005. Bible Footnotes. Pg 793

130 Life Application Study Bible. THE HOLY BIBLE, NEW INTERNATIONAL VERSION ®. Carol Stream. Tyndale House Publishers, Inc. 2005. Pg 825

131 Hybels, Bill. Too Busy Not To Pray; Slowing Down To Be With God. Downers Grove. InterVarsity Press. 1998. Pg 56

132 Arthur, Kay. Lord, Teach Me To Pray In 28 Days. Eugene. Harvest House Publishers. 2008. Pg 29

133 Arthur, Kay. Lord, Teach Me To Pray In 28 Days. Eugene. Harvest House Publishers. 2008. Pg 34

134 Hybels, Bill. Too Busy Not To Pray; Slowing Down To Be With God. Downers Grove. InterVarsity Press. 1998. Pg 55

135 Galli, Mark & Bell, James S. The Complete Idiots Guide To Prayer. New York. Alpha Books. 2004. Pg 94

136 Bounds, E.M. The Complete Works Of E.M. Bounds On Prayer. Grand Rapids. Baker Books. 1990. Pg 338

137 Wilkinson, Bruce. The Prayer Of Jabez. Sisters. Multnomah Publishers, Inc. 2000.

138 Butler, Trent. Holman Illustrated Bible Dictionary. Nashville. Holman Bible Publishers. 2003. Pg 223

139 Wilkinson, Bruce. The Prayer Of Jabez. Sisters. Multnomah Publishers, Inc. 2000. Pgs 86-87

140 Young, Sarah. Jesus Calling. Nashville. Thomas Nelson. 2004. Pg 344

141 Life Application Study Bible. THE HOLY BIBLE, NEW INTERNATIONAL VERSION ®. Carol Stream. Tyndale House Publishers, Inc. 2005. Pg 832

142 Young, Sarah. Jesus Calling. Nashville. Thomas Nelson. 2004. Pg 8

143 Bounds, E. M. The Power Of Prayer. Christian Art Gifts. 2007. April 18

144 Life Application Study Bible. THE HOLY BIBLE, NEW INTERNATIONAL VERSION ®. Carol Stream. Tyndale House Publishers, Inc. 2005. Pg 826

145 Bounds, E. M. The Power Of Prayer. Christian Art Gifts. 2007. April 26

146 Tiegreen, Chris. One Year Devotional: Worship The King. Carol Stream. Tyndale House Publishers, Inc. 2008. March 27. Pg 185

147 Bounds, E. M. The Power Of Prayer. Christian Art Gifts. 2007. April 2

148 Bounds, E.M. The Complete Works Of E.M. Bounds On Prayer. Grand Rapids. Baker Books. 1990. Pg 99

149 Our Daily Bread Daily Devotional. Grand Rapids. RBC Ministries. 1.20.2013

150 Ten Ways To Pray. Cincinnati. Forward Movement Publications. 2010. Pg 3-4

151 French, R.M. The Way Of A Pilgrim. New York. Seabury Press. 1965

152 Galli, Mark & Bell, James S. The Complete Idiots Guide To Prayer. New York. Alpha Books. 2004. Pg 256-257

153 www.goarch.org

154 Munroe, Myles. Understanding The Purpose And Power Of Prayer. New Kensington. Whitaker House. 2002. Pg 41

155 Bounds, E.M. The Complete Works Of E.M. Bounds On Prayer. Grand Rapids. Baker Books. 1990. Pg 460

156 Young, Sarah. Jesus Calling. Nashville. Thomas Nelson. 2004. Pg 5

157 Young, Sarah. Jesus Calling. Nashville. Thomas Nelson. 2004. Pg 110 / 84

158 Exley, Patterson, Hummel, Edwards. Daybreak With God. Tulsa. Honor Books. 1999. Pg 144

159 Our Daily Bread Daily Devotional. Grand Rapids. RBC Ministries. 1.17.2013

160 Cymbala, Jim. Breakthrough Prayer. Grand Rapids. Zondervan. 2003. Pg 83

161 Bounds, E. M. The Power Of Prayer. Christian Art Gifts. 2007. February 10

162 Munroe, Myles. Understanding The Purpose And Power Of Prayer. New Kensington. Whitaker House. 2002. Pg 223

163 Munroe, Myles. Understanding The Purpose And Power Of Prayer. New Kensington. Whitaker House. 2002. Pg 226

164 Damazio,Frank. Season of Intercession. Portland. City Bible Publishing. 1998. Pg 164

165 Wagner, Richard. Christian Prayer For Dummies. New York. Wiley Publishing, Inc. 2003. Pg 136

[166] NIV Archeological Study Bible. Grand Rapids. The Zondervan Corporation. 2005. Bible Footnotes. Pg 1569

[167] Hybels, Bill. Too Busy Not To Pray; Slowing Down To Be With God. Downers Grove. InterVarsity Press. 1998. Pg 147

[168] www.Christianitytoday.com

[169] Wagner, Richard. Christian Prayer For Dummies. New York. Wiley Publishing, Inc. 2003. Pg 121

[170] Ten Ways To Pray. Cincinnati. Forward Movement Publications. 2010. Pg 5

[171] Wagner, Richard. Christian Prayer For Dummies. New York. Wiley Publishing, Inc. 2003. Pg 123

[172] Wagner, Richard. Christian Prayer For Dummies. New York. Wiley Publishing, Inc. 2003. Pg 131

[173] Vann, Gerald. British Theologian. 1906-1963

[174] Tiegreen, Chris. One Year Devotional: Worship The King. Carol Stream. Tyndale House Publishers, Inc. 2008. March 27. Pg 6

[175] Tiegreen, Chris. One Year Devotional: Worship The King. Carol Stream. Tyndale House Publishers, Inc. 2008. April 25. Pg 115

[176] Stanley, Charles F. In Touch. Atlanta. In Touch Ministries. 2013.

[177] Tiegreen, Chris. Creative Prayer. Colorado Springs. Multnomah Books. 2007. Pg 116

[178] Tiegreen, Chris. One Year Devotional: Worship The King. Carol Stream. Tyndale House Publishers, Inc. 2008. April 25. March 3

[179] Life Application Study Bible. THE HOLY BIBLE, NEW INTERNATIONAL VERSION ®. Carol Stream. Tyndale House Publishers, Inc. 2005. Pg 838

[180] LaHaye, Tim and Jenkins, Jerry. John's Story: The Last Eye Witness. New York. G. P. Putnam's Sons. 2006. Pg 159

2y wide side
3y front

working with women
around the world
basic needs
sonya ADRA
www.ADRA.org
1 800 424 2372

877-753-8777
Let's Pray

www women
adventist.org
14 lessons about
women
Luke 1:35

CPSIA information can be obtained
at www.ICGtesting.com
Printed in the USA
FSOW01n1950031214
3691FS